Praise for *God's Many Voices*

"Many people claim to 'hear God's voice,' though not always with discernment. I've found Liz Ditty to be a trustworthy guide in learning how to listen, and how to do so with wise discernment."

Philip Yancey
Best-selling author

"Through beautifully told personal stories of growing to trust the God Who is love, *God's Many Voices* invites us to notice the One who 'has left invisible Post-it Notes for you on the sunrise and throughout your interrupted day.' Reading this wise and engaging book is like spending time with a friend. Liz Ditty encourages us to recognize God's voice by showing us how she has learned to do so: slowly and carefully, with Scripture and loved ones, through thin seasons and thick, and with thanks to good-humored resilience and heaps of grace."

Susan S. Phillips, Ph.D.
Executive director and professor at New College Berkeley
(Graduate Theological Union) and author of *The Cultivated Life*

"Learning to listen to God can, in some ways, mimic learning to ride a bike. We need the mechanics explained, and it's also helpful to have someone running alongside. For novice and experienced riders alike, Liz Ditty provides practical help in hearing God's many voices. Even more importantly, Ditty inspires the thrill of God's company. The one-of-a-kind *God's Many Voices* is sure to become a trusted resource for many."

Jen Pollock Michel
Author of *Keeping Place* and *Teach Us to Want*

"I have a better language, approach, and understanding of God's voice because of this book. Liz Ditty has given us a gift that helps us cut through the noise to hear from the one voice that matters. With humor and rich storytelling, *God's Many Voices* brings us into the nuanced and mysterious, yet ordinary and accessible, world of a speaking God. Ditty reveals what we've always hoped were true: it is possible to hear from God—and we can all listen in."

Chris Nye

Pastor and author of *Distant God*

"In a world with so many channels vying for our attention, God's voice is often shut out by a perpetual stream of noise. Yet, as Liz Ditty so thoughtfully teaches us, if we are mindful and intentional we can begin to discern, attune, and respond to God's voice in our individual lives. Liz's beautiful book is a personal and practical journey that feels like a feast for the soul. Her intimate writing style intertwines the perfect amount of deep theological insight in everyday conversation. *God's Many Voices* is a must-read for anyone longing to grow deeper in their faith and eagerness to understand and hear the voice of God. I devoured this book and plan to return to it again and again."

Lee Wolfe Blum

Speaker, mental health practitioner,

and author of *Brave Is the New Beautiful*

"Liz Ditty believes she hears the voice of God in everyday experiences, and that we can too. Her wise and faithful teaching invites us to find God in the beauty and mess of our ordinary lives, inspiring us to see sacredness all around. *God's Many Voices* reminds us that God can and does speak to all of us, right where we are."

Catherine McNiel

Author of *Long Days of Small Things*

"Liz Ditty writes with gentleness, insight, and grace about a topic that has the potential to divide and confuse us all. To read this book is to give yourself a chance to process what it means to hear from God, and to gain some practical direction on what a life of hearing from God might look like. Filled to overflowing with honesty and transparency, *God's Many Voices* is worth your time and engagement. A true joy to read."

Casey Tygrett

Author of *Becoming Curious*

and host of the *otherWISE* podcast

"In a winsome, approachable style, Liz Ditty teaches and encourages us to freely express ourselves to the Lord and to listen attentively, expecting to hear from Him. Brimming with stories and insights, this book is a delightful guide to developing a rich, conversational relationship with God. *God's Many Voices* will be a trusted companion for many as they learn to notice, discern, and respond to the loving voice of God."

Richella Parham

Author of *A Spiritual Formation Primer*

and vice-chair of Renovaré board of trustees

"*God's Many Voices* is illuminating, especially for those of us who desperately long to hear from God. I put the book down several times in order to ponder the truths Liz Ditty communicates. It invited me to look at myself, my life with God, and Christian community in a new way. Liz makes a difficult topic easier to understand and also relatable. That is truly a feat. I was convicted. And I can say that God spoke to me through this book. It has been one of his many voices in my life."

Marlena Graves

Author of *A Beautiful Disaster*

"Though I do indeed want all people to know Christ, even more I want Christ to be made known. And because He is found everywhere in life, in all places, in all things, I am not just freed but compelled to discover Him through all the lovely, hideous, fascinating things of this world, which are, after all, His. I'm so thankful for Liz Ditty, who invites us all to hear God's many voices outside the church walls to make God known for the loving, communicative God He is."

Leslie Leyland Fields

Author of *Crossing the Waters*

"Our God speaks, in a variety of different ways. I'm grateful for Liz Ditty, who in *God's Many Voices* illuminates a diversity of ways Jesus loves to communicate with us as His people and invites us to listen for His voice like we are expecting to hear it."

Joshua Ryan Butler

A pastor of Redemption Church (Tempe, AZ) and author of *The Skeletons in God's Closet* and *The Pursuing God*

"Liz Ditty writes with warmth, humor, and grace about the spiritual practices that too often feel overwhelming. She approaches the spiritual life with simplicity and generosity and tells a story of learning to listen to the voice of God that inspires me to do the same. *God's Many Voices* is a book for anyone who believes God is still speaking, and anyone who needs a friend to walk them directly toward that Holy Voice."

Micha Boyett

Author of *Found: A Story of Questions, Grace, and Everyday Prayer*

GOD'S
MANY
VOICES

GOD'S MANY VOICES

LEARNING *to* LISTEN

EXPECTANT *to* HEAR

LIZ DITTY

WORTHY®
PUBLISHING

Published by Worthy Books, an imprint of Worthy Publishing Group, a division of Worthy Media, Inc., One Franklin Park, 6100 Tower Circle, Suite 210, Franklin, TN 37067.

WORTHY is a registered trademark of Worthy Media, Inc.

Helping people experience the heart of God

eBook available wherever digital books are sold.

Library of Congress Cataloging-in-Publication Data

Names: Ditty, Liz, author.
Title: God's many voices : learning to listen, expectant to hear / Liz Ditty.
Description: Franklin, TN : Worthy Publishing, 2018.
Identifiers: LCCN 2018022250 | ISBN 9781683972525 (tradepaper)
Subjects: LCSH: Discernment (Christian theology) | Listening—Religious
  aspects—Christianity. | God (Christianity)—Knowableness.
Classification: LCC BV4509.5 .D58 2018 | DDC 248.4—dc23
LC record available at https://lccn.loc.gov/2018022250

For foreign and subsidiary rights, contact rights@worthypublishing.com

Published in association with Don Gates of the literary agency The Gates Group, www.the-gates-group.com.

ISBN: 978-1-68397-252-5

Cover Design: Matt Smartt, Smartt Guys Design
Interior Design and Typesetting: Bart Dawson

Printed in the United States of America
18 19 20 21 22 BP 8 7 6 5 4 3 2 1

Ascribe to the LORD, you heavenly beings,
    ascribe to the LORD glory and strength.
Ascribe to the LORD the glory due his name;
    worship the LORD in the splendor of his holiness.

The voice of the LORD is over the waters;
    the God of glory thunders,
    the LORD thunders over the mighty waters.
The voice of the LORD is powerful;
    the voice of the LORD is majestic.
The voice of the LORD breaks the cedars;
    the LORD breaks in pieces the cedars of Lebanon.
He makes Lebanon leap like a calf,
    Sirion like a young wild ox.
The voice of the LORD strikes
    with flashes of lightning.
The voice of the LORD shakes the desert;
    the LORD shakes the Desert of Kadesh.
The voice of the LORD twists the oaks
    and strips the forests bare.
And in his temple all cry, "Glory!"

The LORD sits enthroned over the flood;
    the LORD is enthroned as King forever.
The LORD gives strength to his people;
    the LORD blesses his people with peace.

—PSALM 29

God has many voices.
May we learn to hear them all.

CONTENTS

FOREWORD

Outside of the Bible, no book has changed me more than Dallas Willard's *The Spirit of the Disciplines*. I contacted Dallas after having read it, and—for no particular reason—he invited me to his Southern California home. I experienced there what countless others have: the unhurried, humble, selfless attention of a human being who lived deeply in the genuine awareness of the reality of the kingdom of God.

Dallas's legacy casts a vision of the nature of the gospel and the kingdom and moral and spiritual truth that is helping the church, which is always reforming to recapture something of the spirit and message of Jesus. Dallas's work, more than that of anyone I know in our day, is helping us understand more clearly the offer of Jesus, about whom Dallas never ceased to marvel. His influence will ripple along in countless sermons and books and churches and disciples.

When I was introduced to Liz Ditty, I was happy to discover the ripples of Dallas's impact continuing to spread. I didn't meet Liz personally while she attended the church I began leading over a decade ago, but she had also learned about Dallas and his work. Liz left church one Sunday and asked a bookstore employee down the road if they had any books written by Dallas Willard.

That employee handed her a copy of *Hearing God*, and she experienced the same radical life changes that I had encountered through Dallas's words long before. Liz's faith, fragile from years of spiritual abuse, came to life when she learned that God doesn't just speak to the spiritually elite or professional church leaders—He speaks to all of us, in so many ways.

God is stretching Himself toward us, waiting for us to notice the words He has been whispering all along. He wants us to live our life with Him—even (especially) the ordinary parts. The central promise of the Bible is not "I will forgive you"; the best promise in the Bible is "I will be with you." Our individual uniqueness means we will all experience God's presence and learn to relate to Him in different ways. A strong foundation underlies the diverse ways that God speaks to us and the unique paths that lead us toward His voice.

Foundational truths of my life with God are:

- God is always present and active in my life, whether or not I see Him.
- Coming to recognize and experience God's presence is a learned behavior—I can cultivate it.
- My task is to meet God in this moment.
- I am always tempted to live "outside" this moment. When I do that, I lose my sense of God's presence.
- Sometimes God seems far away for reasons I do not understand. Those moments, too, are opportunities to learn.
- Whenever I fail, I can always start again right away. No one knows the full extent to which a human being can experience God's presence.

- My desire for God ebbs and flows, but His desire for me is constant.
- Every thought carries a "spiritual charge" that moves me a little closer to, or a little farther from, God.
- Every aspect of my life-work, relationships, hobbies, errands . . . is of immense and genuine interest to God.
- My path to experiencing God's presence will not look quite like anyone else's.
- Straining and trying hard do not help.

Your life with God is waiting for you. God is running toward you, now and always. There is no better time to listen for His voice than in this moment. I believe this can be the greatest moment of your life, because this moment is the place where you can meet with God. In fact, this moment is the only place where you can meet God.

You can learn to listen for God's voice and to hear Him more clearly each time. The same God who is within us is also all about us. He is not restricted to church or the Bible. He speaks in many voices, and we can expect that what He has to say is very, very good.

—John Ortberg
Senior pastor of Menlo Church and author of
I'd Like You More If You Were More Like Me

A NEW, FAMILIAR VOICE

Thinking back to God's first words to me, they were not as kind as I would have scripted. . . .

I was thirteen years old, very awake in the dark of night, lying on the top bunk bed. My younger sister, still in elementary school, was tucked beneath her covers in the bunk below. Although I could only faintly hear her rhythmic breathing, her soundness of sleep emanated through her pale, freckled skin and pink sheets and up the very posts of the bed we shared. Lying anxious and alert, I was unable—or maybe unwilling—to let my eyes close.

I couldn't stop staring at an orange glow on the ceiling that had a bit of dance to its shadow. It was strangely warmer than the light normally put off by our little night light, as though it were a reflection from a flame. The inner voice that had narrated the first decade or so of my life was busy rambling, frustrated and confused because my dad asked me earlier that day if I was a Christian. He should know. He clapped when I received my Bible memorization trophies, and it was no secret I had asked Jesus to save me from my sins—well, to save me from hell—probably a few hundred times.

I stared at my hand in front of my face, fingers splayed open, and tried to see double. That usually helped me calm down.

If my dad didn't know, how could I know if I was a Christian? Everything I thought I was supposed to do, he had watched me do.

"You don't know Me."

The words came suddenly, jolting my inner dialogue.

I thought immediately of a verse I had learned in Sunday school about people calling Jesus "Lord" and His saying, "I never knew you" (see Matthew 7:21–23). I knew a lot about Jesus and the Bible. I had studied Greek and Hebrew dictionaries before I owned my first lip gloss. How could I not know Him?

My father was an influential elder in a hyperlegalistic church that functioned more like a cult. The church called itself The Assembly. It prided itself on having many elders, not just one pastor. In reality it was one elder, my dad's best friend, who actually held all the power. He and my dad and another elder met to discuss the state of the church regularly, and that included the details of everyone's life. They arranged marriages, made college and career decisions, oversaw relationships with friends and family, and were also involved in the personal financial decisions of church members. There were no areas in which they did not have input. All of us were accountable to their peering eyes, and their wisdom carried the weight of divine appointment. The elders told us that God had entrusted them with all of our lives, like shepherds over His flock. God gave them His authority and guidance, and He spoke to them regularly. All we had to do was ask them what God said.

The elders were the interpreters of Scripture and the enforcers of the rules. Whenever the church was officially gathered, the women had to be completely silent unless they were joining to sing a hymn. Women also needed to wear a veil, or head covering, as an outward symbol of their inward submission to the men and to God. The veil was worn at all church gatherings but also at home during personal devotion time. I had one made of ivory lace. Modesty was paramount, and I was taught from an early age how seductive my skin was. High necks as well as covered shoulders and knees were required at all times—and nothing clinging to the form of my body.

It slowly dawned on me in college that 99 percent of Christian women did not wear long skirts or head veils. Though I had been taught that we were the only "true believers" who honored Scripture instead of being swept up in worldly culture, I began to study the Bible more voraciously on my own. I went to a very conservative college, and most of the girls at my school also wore head coverings. The strict Assembly I went to was a small offshoot of an offshoot, but this college somehow gathered a couple hundred students with similar backgrounds from across the United States and Canada. It was within my first weeks away from home, when I was settling into my strictly all-female dorm, that I was given the wrong student work assignment that would supplement my tuition. Most freshmen got kitchen jobs, but by some strange fluke I was assigned a job usually reserved for seniors: I showed up for my first day as library proctor, the librarian's assistant.

I can picture myself in that library, hiding behind the exposed pipes in an area off to the side where there was more space so I could pull tables together. I regularly abandoned the front reception desk where most of the other proctors would sit doing their homework. I stacked books upon books, some open to certain pages and turned over on other open books only to be anchored down by a closed book I hadn't read yet on the top. Index cards stuck out of books, and a small stack of rejected books sat off to the side. The library was usually empty and always quiet, smells mixing from books, dust piled on untrafficked shelves, and the odor of a musty basement. I started wearing a bandana as a more fashionable, less obvious head covering.

It was when I pored over the worn pages of those aged books— commentaries on 1 Corinthians 11 and the end times—that my world came crashing in around me. Some published works documented what I had been taught, but most of my piles and stacks definitively disproved the theories I had been trained to defend. My dad was wrong. The elders were wrong. I was wrong. I started hyperventilating.

Through a special kind of grace, as my entire universe was spinning around me and beginning to crumble, I heard the echo of God's words to me years before: "You don't know Me."

And I realized God wasn't disowning me.

His words were an invitation, not an accusation.

He was inviting me into a freedom that I hadn't learned yet. When I first heard those words as a child, I had imagined being in a crowd and screaming out to Jesus, only to have Him look at me with narrow eyes and slowly say, "You don't know Me" before He turned to walk away. When these same words came back to me a decade later, I finally understood how Jesus was actually saying them. He was saying them softly, over and over, holding me tightly as I sobbed fearful, angry tears in that library. I still had a lot to learn about Him.

After college, I left our Assembly and was shut out of the lives of pretty much everyone I had ever known. My dad should have taken a harder line to cut off his rebellious daughter (a term that had been reserved for my younger sister up to this point), but it turned out he loved me. And I loved him. That made everything infinitely more complicated, more painful, and more tolerable at the same time. Those last couple years—which we didn't know would be our last ones together—were actually pretty sweet. I would visit my parents' house for dinner and agree not to talk about anything but eggplant parmesan and good places to get a pedicure. Once or twice I could have sworn my dad was actually deeply proud of me. He died when I was twenty-five.

Over the next decade I searched for the Jesus I wanted to know. I looked in different denominations and at different authors and teachers. I found myself at a Presbyterian church in Menlo Park, learning from their new pastor, John Ortberg. He talked about a man he had learned a lot from named Dallas Willard, so I went to a local bookstore and found his book titled *Hearing God*. That was when I first realized that God was talking to me, straight to me, and I didn't need people who were more authoritative or famous or spiritual to tell me what He was saying. No middleman required, I could live my best life in God's company.

I didn't need the elders to tell me where God wanted me to go to school or whom I should marry; all of these decisions and all of life was now an adventure I could take with God. Surprisingly, it was harder than I thought not to have someone telling me what God wanted me to do. I discovered that the cultlike devotion that had been previously demanded of me was far easier for me to transfer to good pastors or celebrity Christians than I thought. It's convenient to hear "what God says" in social media one-liners or quotable taglines in the foreground of beautiful images—but He has so much more to say to us! Gently, many times, God has reminded me that He isn't inviting me to follow good teachers and good churches, but that good teachers and good churches are at their best when they help me follow Him.

When Jesus invited the disciples to follow Him, He invited them to learn from Him, to eat with Him, to walk with Him, to listen to His stories and to tell Him theirs. He's inviting us to the same conversational relationship, the same way to know Him. Jesus tells His stories in lots of different ways and in many voices that we can hear if we're paying attention. And Jesus has left invisible Post-it Notes for you on the sunrise and throughout your interrupted day. His words are waiting for you on the thin pages of your Bible, in the mouth of your child, and even in the song that comes on the loudspeaker at the grocery store. This book is about learning to recognize God's voice. About being awake to how God is already extending Himself toward us.

> Jesus invited the disciples . . . to learn from Him, to eat with Him, to walk with Him, to listen to His stories and to tell Him theirs. He's inviting us to the same conversational relationship.

Did you know that scientists believe the stars make sounds like instruments or singing? They are still learning how to listen for that sound through the vast space and dark vacuum between us and the distant lights. Because they now expect to hear something, they are listening and developing tools for greater awareness. My prayer is that as we listen together, the divine Voice would have its unharnessed role in our lives, singing wildly like the constellations of the night sky over a desert. A voice that's always been there, that we are just beginning to hear.

Now when I hear God whisper, "You don't know Me," it sounds almost playful. He's inviting all of us to know Him better and experience Him more. God has words for His world, for His people, and just for you. His whispers are carried by His Spirit, riding on the wind, making themselves known to ears that hear. God has something to say. God is speaking to each of us, and all of us are able to hear Him.

PART ONE

LEARNING TO LISTEN

CHAPTER 1

NOTICING GOD'S WHISPERS

I didn't pack anything to go to the beach that morning. It had been a slow, blurry week with nothing but exhaustion and uncertainty over why little things felt so hard. I turned the key in the ignition and drove to meet God. I didn't tell Him I was coming, but Jesus promised that He always answers the door. I needed a getaway, some inspiration, some God-strength to get me through. Pulling out of the driveway, I had a thrilling rush, as if I were starting a yearlong journey around the world with nothing but the clothes on my back. My lips tightened into the sideways smirk they make when I am doing something unexpected and a little irresponsible.

The beach is just far enough away to be a trip, but still close enough to be a friend. As the road lengthened in my rearview mirror, I thought I could outrun my racing mind, but I am harder to get away from than I expected. Head buzzing with hypothetical conversations and unlikely situations and very real strategic plans to conquer the week ahead, I kept interrupting myself to announce, "Almost there now. The beach will clear my mind."

I opened the car door and stepped out into clean oxygen, bright sunshine, and the smell of salt. I wanted the fragrant breeze to blow its sticky wildness around every strand of my hair. *Hello, God. Here I am.* The sidewalk was peppered with stray sand as every step took me farther into the piercing blue sky, the skin-warming sun, and the spirit-soothing breeze. I laid my sweatshirt on the impressionable dune and sat down, sinking in. *Okay, God . . .*

I didn't actually have a plan, and it seemed a very normal day at the beach. I don't think I expected angels to greet me, but whatever I expected, this actual moment was not as spiritual as I had hoped it would be. . . . I don't like sitting down for very long, so I hopped up with a new idea: walking.

I tied my sweatshirt around my waist, picked up my sandals by their thin straps, and went down to the water where the sea-foam teases, then surges. Everything was beautiful, everything was right, but everything was still just a beach.

I started to question what I was even waiting for, what I was expecting, what it even means for God to "show up." I breathed, deeply. I even opened my arms up and lifted my sandals high above my head with a slow and exaggerated inhale. I sighed my breath out with a defeated exhale. My hands fell. *I'm not doing this right. Nothing's happening.*

I had been intentional about making time to be with God, but I couldn't get comfortable in the quiet of my escape. Pressure, fear, and fatigue were all still screaming at me, and everything inside my brain that kept me from connecting with God at home had followed me to the beach. I stared down the gorgeous coastline and tried to pray, catching myself again and again lost in my own wandering thoughts and distractions. I felt I was talking to the sky.

I was losing my train of thought . . . underwhelmed . . . hearing nothing but the wind in response.

That's when I lost my breath for a split second while staring at the surface of the ocean's gliding, piling waves. A rush of wind caught my imagination up in wondering what lies below and beyond the surface of those shimmering sunlight and blue-gray shadows. What all is going on in the ocean today? God told Job that He knows where sea monsters sleep. I wondered how far away that underwater cave might be and if the mythic Leviathan was still there resting. *Give me a hint, God.*

My prayers were changing.

NASA says that we have better maps of the surface of the moon and Mars than we do of the ocean floor. God explained Himself to Job by owning the mysteries of

> I started to question what I was even waiting for, what I was expecting, what it even means for God to "show up."

the ocean, and I let myself fall into those mysteries. Wrapped in wonder, I started to see Him too. *If He is truly present everywhere, even in undiscovered corners of the dark ocean floor, He must be present here with me now. Whether or not I can feel Him, whether or not I can focus my attention, He is here. If He knows where the Leviathan sleeps, He knows where His daughter stands.*

I finally heard God's voice whispering, a force pulling, from just beyond the scattered distractions that had slyly followed me to the beach. "Don't be afraid. I am with you."

That was it. One little catch of breath. One simple thought of involuntary worship. Awareness of my smallness giving me incredible respect for God's being. He hadn't finally ridden up on a wave like King Triton. Instead, He had patiently and kindly touched my eyes with salty grace for one moment, and I saw that my awareness of His presence had been too easily uncalibrated. He is mysterious and big, and He doesn't live at the beach. He is always present with me and usually closer and more available than I dare to imagine.

God, give me eyes to see. Ears that hear. A heart that never loses its sense of wonder.

Sacred space in the Old Testament, holy ground, was a place where God and humans met. Moments before the meeting, before shoes were taken off and bodies fell flat before Him, holy ground was ordinary, dusty, rocky earth. But that is exactly where God meets us, right here in our world. On our dusty, rocky planet.

A Samaritan woman met Jesus by a dusty well on the wrong side of the tracks in John 4. She asked Jesus which mountain to climb to meet with God. Jesus tenderly told her a shocking truth: one day soon everyone would worship God in Spirit, not in a temple or on a mountain. The apostle Paul picked up Jesus's thought and explained that the holy, official place where the Divine interacted with humans—the temple—wasn't a place or a building anymore. Our very bodies are God's temple.

> Our own skin, with all its susceptibility and strangeness, forms the walls of a sacred space—our very selves—where God meets humanity. Where God meets us.

All of my chaos may have followed me to the beach, but so did all of my capacity to meet God just as I am. My body is a temple; your body is a temple if you have offered it to God. Our own skin, with all its susceptibility and strangeness, forms the walls of a sacred space—our very selves—where God meets humanity. Where

God meets us. Holy ground is under the soles of our feet always. God's Spirit isn't a pilgrimage away, or hovering distant and uninterested in a far corner of the universe, or in a vault that only special people have the code to unlock. If we belong to God, we carry His Spirit with us. Within us.

When I don't know what to pray and have almost forgotten that I am God's child, I hold on to that reality and this truth: I am not far from God, and He is not far from me. The space my body occupies is a meeting place with God. From the first days God created humans, He has walked and talked with us. It's what He loves to do. We were designed with the capacity to talk with God, because He's always intended to love us and be with us.

As much as the possibilities of intelligent design excite me, they can be incredibly intimidating. The camera store in our neighborhood had a vendor fair around the time I was thinking of buying a camera. All of the big companies had banners with their logos hanging over the front of tables covered with black tablecloths and manned by sales reps. Spread out on the table were different lenses and filters and various parts scattered between them. One of the reps was all smiles as he called out for me to come see one of his cameras. He gingerly passed it to me, and my hands fumbled. "Oh, wow. I didn't realize cameras were so heavy."

He explained to me how the camera was built and the internal lenses and something about shutter speed and light. I didn't want to interrupt him—he was really on a roll—but when he flipped the camera around to show me how to change the aperture and other settings, I finally came clean.

"Look, I'm not a photographer. I just want a camera that won't take blurry pictures. Do you have one with a good auto mode?"

He blinked at me three times and smiled with his eyes wide as if he was about to say something obvious: "If you want pictures that aren't blurry, you should learn to use the settings."

That sounded complicated, so I thanked him and went to the next table. But I kept thinking about what he said.

You see, we're all living in these temple bodies that are capable of hearing God and talking to Him. Like my camera and me, though, most of us leave our fullest capabilities to the experts. We don't know where to start because we don't understand all of the factors and settings. Overwhelmed, we can't imagine how minor adjustments will make that much of a difference anyway. Not to mention, I'm a little lazy.

Yet God's intention from the very beginning—evident in the first days of Eden—was to be in conversational relationship with humans. He didn't abandon that goal after our rebellion. He made promises, vows, and covenants to rescue and restore humans to their design, with the intention of us being with Him and hearing His voice.

With the Bible so adamantly insisting that God is speaking to us, and always has been, why do so few of us recognize God's voice in our daily lives?

Learning to listen is about noticing all the things God is already saying to us that we may not be hearing. Listening can be just as valuable as hearing. We may find different spiritual seasons of our life dominated more by hearing or by listening. Even when we can't hear God, we can lean forward and try to notice and listen. We'll learn that silence is part of the ongoing conversation between God and man, with its own purpose. Our engagement with God is what matters. Whether we are in the depths of doubt or enjoying a keen awareness of His voice, the goal of listening is not simply to hear God's words but to move closer to Him.

How we view ourselves also matters to our relationship with God. It is difficult to notice God when we are occupied with numbing our emotions or pain. In her book *The Gifts of Imperfection*, Brené Brown points out, "We cannot selectively numb emotions. When we numb the painful emotions, we also numb the positive emotions." The same low points that send us seeking after God's comforting voice can prompt us to unhealthy comforts as well. Dysfunctional relationships, shopping, food, alcohol, technology, and other distractions not only keep us busy and a little satisfied, but they also keep us completely stuck.

> Learning to listen is about noticing all the things God is already saying to us that we may not be hearing. Listening can be just as valuable as hearing.

Sometimes, without realizing it, we get in our own way of hearing God's voice. Once we know what to listen for, we can get ready to listen. When the Bible talks about eyes that see God and ears that hear God, those abilities are linked to our heart (Isaiah 6:10; John 12:39–41). We find it difficult to hear God's voice when we allow bitterness, unforgiveness, or anger to slowly harden our hearts. In Matthew 5:23–24 Jesus taught that if we are angry with someone or if someone is angry with us, it's better to leave our sacrifice at the base of the altar, go to be reconciled, then come back to worship God. If we feel awkward in our conversation with God, we can also take inventory of our relationships with other people. Our hardness toward other people can harden our heart to God.

You may not think you've heard from God lately, but you may not have known what to listen for. When we think about hearing God's voice, our first picture can be something like clouds parting, total clarity, and an audible voice that thunders something important. God can speak like that, but that's not His only voice. Burning bushes and clouds of fire have held the voice of God, but so have whispers and silently overflowing jars of oil.

God loves to break into our ordinary. He loves to meet us where we are, as we are. He loves to join us on our favorite couch early in the morning as we pore over His Words, or sing softly to Him in the kitchen during the day, or toss restlessly in our bed at night. Conversation with God is not merely an exchange of words or receiving directions; it's an ongoing conversation that develops intimacy and connection.

Have you ever been driving, worried sick about something, and then had your breath taken away by the sunset? God loves to remind us of how big He and His world are so we can gain perspective on our problems.

Have you ever seen someone and just known you were supposed to talk to him or her? God nudges us toward one another.

Have you ever come across words in the Bible or on a billboard and felt as though they were put there for you, for that exact moment? God leaves us notes in the most surprising places.

You can hear God. You probably already have.

Even when we clearly hear God's voice, it can be difficult to own that truth for ourselves. It's hard to trust the voice of God when so many who hear God speak hear Him say the strangest things or think everything they encounter is God's affirmation of their own plans. I know a man who claimed God told him to leave his wife and children for another woman, a soul mate whom God had designed just for him. I listened to an interview with a Nazi who was an active member in the Ku Klux Klan, and he quoted Scripture—God's own words—cherry-picked and misinterpreted to justify his hate, racism, and violence. Self-delusion loves divine approval.

The only thing worse than a church of people who hear God say crazy things is a church of people who aren't listening for His voice at all.

So we walk toward this holy conversation with God knowing that our self-deception follows us like a shadow. Still, we cannot opt out. If we say we follow Jesus, we have to follow Him. We have to have a relationship with Him that goes beyond transactional morality and that more closely mirrors how He wants to relate to us: as a brother (Hebrews 2:11), a friend (John 15:15), and even a newlywed (2 Corinthians 11:2). No relationship can thrive without communication, and our relationship with God is no different.

Now, I'd love to say that I've never put words in God's mouth or chosen to misunderstand what He was saying, but I've done both. It's hard when God isn't saying what I want to hear. During my career transition from a high-tech company into motherhood, for instance, I hit a point where I was desperate to know what was next. I couldn't tell if my break from the workforce was temporary or if God was leading me through this big transition into new territory. I had left a job that I loved: amazing coworkers, meaningful work, and the invigorating sense that I brought unique value to our team.

Still, here I was, obeying what I thought was God's voice directing me to take a break—and I was miserable. I loved my baby, but I was battling depression and utterly humbled by how hard it was to be a mom at home. Not only was it mentally difficult to be in such a thankless and unseen role, but it felt physically impossible to feed my child and keep my house clean—and don't even talk to me about the gym. I had always been a competent achiever in school and work, but motherhood kicked my tail. I prayed every day for weeks about going back to work. Hearing nothing but silence in response, I reluctantly took the advice of a trusted mentor and obeyed the last clear thing I had heard from God: stay at home. I knew I had a lot to be thankful for, and I grudgingly believed— but see clearly now—that God had good things for me in that time.

One day, as I stared into the blank slate of my future, I thought I heard a whisper from God: "Liz, you're not going to teach executives anymore. I want you to teach My people."

I was desperate for new direction, but this had been such a subtle thought in my mind. I wasn't sure if it was God. I asked Him to repeat Himself.

"Was that You?"

Silence.

"Where do I start?"

Silence.

"What exactly am I supposed to do?"

Silence.

Over the next three months, I would wholeheartedly seek God. I prayed. I read my Bible. I asked Him over and over to clarify His words. I looked for opportunities that might be His leading me toward this new thing. I asked the church if they needed help.

Silence.

In my next meeting with my spiritual director, I earnestly described to her how God was teasing and eluding me. I asked if she thought I had heard Him wrong. Or if that was a call on my life, was it for now or for ten years from now? I leaned forward and asked so many questions, not even realizing I wasn't waiting for her to answer a single one.

She took a deep breath.

"Liz, I don't think God is hiding from you. He just isn't where you are looking."

I was confused, and she sensed it. She smiled gently as she asked kindly, "Are you looking for God, or are you looking for answers?"

For the first time that morning, I was silent. My motives always surprise me. It's possible to seek God's voice but not seek God. We won't find Him if we are moving toward our own goals and desires and trying to see Him there. God is who He is, and if we want to hear Him, we have to come to Him in our own broken desire to love Him. Listening should be an act of love, not a grasp for certainty. We have to move only toward Him and His love, not toward His wisdom or blessing or direction.

As I moved toward God during that silent, uncertain season of my life, I didn't make any progress toward what I thought my new calling would be. His silence about my calling directed me to other words He had for me. I ended up needing to take a healing journey before I went on a purpose-seeking adventure. God was so kind, so good, but so direct. I had anger that was covering deep pain. I had pride that had grown into arrogance and insecurity. I had developed unhealthy relationships with food in my quest for comfort and escape. None of this was fun to work through.

Sometimes freedom feels harder than addiction. The call that I thought I may have heard—the plan I wondered if God had for my future—wasn't my direction or my goal for those years. The plan I'd heard earlier became a little gift of grace I held close, a sweet promise that no matter how hard my mess was to deal with, I knew God wasn't done with me yet.

Thankfully, the truth is that if I—if we—have to be in a healthy place before we hear God, we might never hear Him. God has never asked us to clean ourselves up before we come to Him— He knows us too well. He breaks through the silence even when we are in no place to hear Him. One of the clearest encounters with the loudest auditory voice of God in the New Testament was when Saul (who would later become Paul) was on the road to Damascus. He was a Jesus-persecutor. He hunted down Christians to torture and kill them. He could not have been more tuned out, but God broke through.

> It's not the holy ones or the artistic ones or the ones with healthy childhoods who hear the birds sing; it's the listeners who hear. You can hear and see and understand more than you know.

I also would have never heard God's voice if I had to be calm or attentive or humble or patient, because I was none of those things. Those things help us grow into an ongoing conversation and awareness of God's constant presence in our world, but do not be intimidated if they feel unattainable right now. You learn as you practice, but even a child can learn to take a picture with a complex camera.

Once you learn to notice the things in your day that are easy to ignore, you'll notice them more and more. As you learn to recognize what is truly from God and learn how to respond to His goodness and invitations, His voice will shape your life. There is a world of color and smell and sensation waiting to be discovered. It's the world we live in but didn't realize was there. It's not the holy ones or the artistic ones or the ones with healthy childhoods who hear the birds sing; it's the listeners who hear. You can hear and see and understand more than you know. It's a way to live life richly, and it often plays out in the simplest of pleasures. The most ordinary days and thoughts and moments.

God has been walking and talking with humans since the very beginning, and He is still with us—still speaking to us—today. Eden was originally a refuge from chaos, but chaos was invited back in with that first sin and wrapped its dark tendrils around so much of human existence. Underneath that darkness, under the soot of grief and confusion, God's original design is beckoning us. We aren't just capable of talking with God; we were meant to live our lives with Him. On this crazy planet, we can discover God's fingerprints and holy spaces at every turn, where traces of divine love glimmer in the wildest places.

LISTENING FOR
GOD'S VOICE

Consider taking time to process your own journey in a journal. Share with a friend who is a good listener—and listen to their story too.

1. Have you ever been aware of God's voice or presence? What was it like?

2. What do you think God is like, based on your interactions with Him?

3. What do you do when you want to listen for God's voice?

4. On average, how many times during the day do you notice God? What about you, your emotions, your day do you think might change if you noticed Him more?

CHAPTER 2

RECOGNIZING
GOD'S EXPRESSIONS

My dad was dying. For weeks he lay in the center of his living room. There was no bedroom downstairs in my parents' house, so the couch was pushed aside when the hospital bed was brought in, and we all walked past him on our way to get a cup of water or to go to the bathroom. The cancer had been so cruel, but now it was hard to tell if the radiation had been worse. We tried to be casual, tried to pretend we were having a normal conversation with him, as we assessed his decline. But we were too panicked and our voices were too hushed. Once he even rolled his eyes at me.

The air was thick: a thundercloud of grief had already begun descending. It had filled the upstairs where we all hid when we cried, but it was seeping through the floorboards and coming through the ceiling of the living room where Dad was. We were supposed to be strong when we were downstairs. We were supposed to hang on tight and remember every moment of these last days, but we all just wanted to run straight into that thundercloud and be angry and scream and give in to the freedom of collapsing. How were we supposed to treasure this time with him? It was impossible to pretend that we were making memories as we watched his body decay. From the moment of his diagnosis, the brain cancer had taken away his ability to speak coherently, and now he barely made sounds at all. We all sat in the pain of words unsaid and apologies we could no longer expect. It was nothing compared to the intense agony he wore on his face. We held back our resentment and grief with thin smiles as we placed straws between his lips and pleaded with him to drink.

It was early in the evening, and I was in the kitchen opening cupboards and closing them for a reason even I had forgotten. I noticed people walking to the living room, silently, one by one, from all corners of the house. No one said anything. I turned and felt it too. We were all around Dad now, our hands lightly touching the blanket that covered his legs. He didn't look different, he wasn't breathing differently, but something was entirely different. His eyes were closed, and I studied him. He breathed out, slowly, quietly, and he was gone. My eyes scanned from his head to his toes, and there was something strange about his stillness that I can't name, the almost imperceptible difference between sleep and death. On both sides of his bed, all of our hands were still resting on him. An image rushed my memory as I recalled the story of a paralyzed man whose friends had brought him to Jesus. They held on to the sides of his bed and carried him so he could be made whole. When they could not break through the crowd, they tore a hole in the roof and lowered him through the ceiling. I gripped the edge of his hospital blanket tightly. I had just held the side of the bed my dad was lying on when he met Jesus. When his wholeness was restored.

I had always believed people have souls and that these souls live on outside the body after death, waiting for a more complete resurrection. But this belief didn't prepare me for that day, the precise moment, when I saw a body with a soul suddenly be without it. I have never seen a soul as clearly as I did when I was watching that body. The separation of spiritual and physical came completely undone for me. All of our physical see-and-touch world is animated by spiritual realities. I can never unlearn that.

In *Hearing God*, Dallas Willard refers to "the overwhelming presence of the visible world" as one of our greatest barriers to hearing God's voice. The invisibility of the spiritual world invites distrust, so placing too much importance on it feels like a special form of insanity. We all know someone who spiritualizes everything, and the danger of that is obvious, but the danger of spiritualizing nothing is just as real. It's far too easy to forget that we don't live in our own little visible world of commuting and deadlines and relationships and favorite coffee places. We exist in a vast and interconnected world of people and things and places where both heaven and hell come dangerously close to the muddy ground of earth.

The invisibility of the spiritual world invites distrust, so placing too much importance on it feels like a special form of insanity.

We can expect holy moments in living rooms just as often as in church. Over the years as my arms ravaged through darkness for the nearness of God, my fingertips have felt something slide past me, like a dolphin's wet skin, too slippery to grasp. Occasionally, though, my whole fist has grabbed onto something solid and secure. Just as God is "I AM who I AM," His holiness will be what it will be.

We don't always have words for these sacred secrets. And too few people can bridle suspicion and listen with curiosity about our God glances. Even we ourselves hold them lightly and without enough confidence.

We don't always know if it was God's voice we heard. Are we so vain as to think He speaks to us? As Willard further observes in *Hearing God*, "God's spiritual invasions into human life seem, by their very gentleness, to invite us to explain them away."

Yet God is still speaking. He hasn't abandoned His story. He is still actively present and moving in our world. Every story has an arc: a beginning, a middle, and an end. In the beginning God created order and life out of chaos and desolation. Then He walked with humans, taught them how to care for their world, and gave them leadership and stewardship of the earth. God loved these two humans, knew them, and let them know Him. One day the humans decided they didn't need God, His rules, or His advice. They decided they could make their own rules.

This rebellion is sometimes blamed on a woman and a snake, but it has played out a million times in a million ways since then. The "I don't need God's way; I will do it my way" decision is in no way isolated to an ancient garden. Unfortunately, our way never ends well. Each of us has been affected by the bad choices of others; and if we are being very honest, we realize that we, too, have hurt others and our earth in irrevocable ways.

Our world is a broken place that isn't as it should be. But what about this God? Where did He go after the humans rebelled? He stayed. His presence is seamlessly continued in the story after the garden. He gives humanity gifts and opportunities, and He listens to our cries. He begins the central plot struggle—God's reckless, repeated attempts to remake and redeem the story. His all-out pursuit to rescue the people He loves, who don't always want to be rescued. This story that we find ourselves in now is not our quest to find God, but His quest to be found by us.

Jesus left all of heaven to embody God's stop-at-nothing determination to be with us, to love us. Jesus didn't come to condemn us; He came to give us life. To be the ransom that could reunite us with God. And Jesus is coming back again to set everything right.

The bad choices, hatred, racism, violence, and self-centeredness that have nearly destroyed us and our planet are called sin. Sin ruined everything. Christ made change possible. Repentance turns us in the opposite direction as we say, "Not my way, God's way" instead of what comes more naturally to us, "Not God's way! My way." God saved us from our self-destruction so He could be with us. We don't have to wait until we get to heaven; God wants to be with us now, and He is inviting us to enter the story He is still writing here on earth.

> This story that we find ourselves in now is not our quest to find God, but His quest to be found by us.

In other words, eternal life with God starts now.

Although He has many voices and many names, there is only one God and one storyline. He calls Himself "I AM who I AM." A friend of mine loves this name because it means that God is exactly who He is, authentic and truly Himself in every situation. And I love the invitation of the name. When God says, "I'm Me," He invites us to discover more of the infinite nature of who He is in the context of our ongoing relationship with Him. God calls Himself "I AM," and we call Him Healer, Provider, Love, Peace,

Victory, Wisdom, Almighty, Father, Jesus, Brother, Friend, and more names as we discover more of who He is.

This is the story we find ourselves in.

So if we believe that God is who He says He is and that He has plans for the world we live in, it would make no sense for Him to be silent now. God did not leave His Holy Spirit on earth like a watchful Elf on the Shelf. His Spirit is full of power, encouragement, and guidance for His people. For us. For today. Our world is full of the spiritual realities of good and evil that are in constant conflict. The greatest spiritual reality is that God is with us as He always has been.

Of course God is speaking to you. He has been trying to tell you all along who He is, who you are, what you are made for. He has a story He is writing just for you. It's part of His larger story, and He has designed you for a part only you can play. As you navigate your part in God's plan, He has things He'll need to talk to you about.

So how can we really know which words are God's? How do we distinguish between His words and our own thoughts? It's not always easy to tell the difference between the voice of God and other thoughts that bombard us.

Dallas Willard calls out three ways to recognize God's voice: "What we discern when we learn to recognize God's voice in our heart is a certain *weight or force*, a certain *spirit*, and a certain *content* in the thoughts that come in God's communications to us" (*Hearing God*). God's confirmation, Willard teaches, comes through a distinctive spiritual element of God's glory, the Holy Spirit, and Scripture—three lights that can guide us.

God's voice is marked by *His glory*. It's not always a blindingly radiant glory, but it is His unique glory that stands apart. The Greek and Hebrew words used in the Bible to describe God's glory are associated with either weightiness or a shining radiance. We can learn to recognize both the moments God weighs in with His presence and the things that shimmer with His glory.

It's okay to be unsure. Many times something catches me by surprise—an unexpected message, a strong thought, or a song on the radio—and I'm not sure if it's God speaking. The ability to recognize God's plans, words, and actions is called discernment. Sometimes that discernment process has just as much value as the message itself.

There is a story of a young boy named Samuel who heard God but hadn't yet learned to recognize His voice. He lived in the temple, and one night he heard someone calling his name in the night. Immediately, he assumed it was the high priest, Eli. When he went to Eli to see what he wanted, Eli told him, "Go and lie down, and if he calls you, say, 'Speak, LORD, for your servant is listening'" (1 Samuel 3:9). When something strikes me as a potential word from the Lord, I think of it as that voice Samuel heard. Not sure where the voice is coming from, I simply respond prayerfully, "Lord, I'm listening." Just as in the story of Samuel, God will often speak again, and it will more clearly be His voice. Confirmation is an important part of discernment.

The more we hear God call our name, the more we will confidently recognize His distinctive tone of voice. His voice is strong, confident, and sure. The waves and wind obey. It's rarely flowery, but always gentle. Disarming even the most defensive; assuring the fearful. Maybe convicting; never condemning. We learn the tone of God's voice through experience, and by becoming familiar with the words of Jesus in the Gospels. Time, experience, patience, and failure are all important teachers when it comes to recognizing God's tone of voice.

The *Holy Spirit* has creative ways of tapping our shoulder. If we are only listening for God to speak to us in audible words, we will miss most of what He has to say. God speaks to us in many ways, and we learn to recognize the weight or grip a certain word or image has on us. Sometimes the Holy Spirit may speak to us through the simplest images or circumstances. Like walking in the grass.

I was on a walk with my children, and as they ran ahead of me, I was praying through some serious self-doubt. I was working on a project that was beginning to feel unimportant, and my original creative vision of something interesting and world changing was fading fast. So was my enthusiasm. I had already been walking for about a mile on this trail when God suddenly and very sharply drew my attention to the grass. I'd walked past millions of blades of grass already, but I saw the blades in front of me very differently. I felt the Lord telling me that even though everyone comments on the flowers, He still loved creating the grass. Every piece of grass is beautiful, valued, and important in all of its ordinariness.

> Our confidence in God's voice grows the more we listen. Sometimes clarity comes as a complete gift of grace, but we will have more certainty in God's direction the more we intentionally listen to Him every day.

This creative task He had given me was more like grass than wildflowers. It might fade into the background, but that ordinary grass fills our world with gorgeous shades of green. God created the grass, and He was asking me to create something ordinary too. The weight of the image, and the fact that I had never thought of anything like that before, helped me recognize God's voice. I was able to finish my project strong, and I've had a new appreciation since then for "ordinary creation"—if there is such a thing.

The *content* of the message can also reveal the messenger. What God says is always consistent with His values, character, and directions that are clearly expressed in the Bible. God does not tell you that you should take that thing from work because you are underpaid: He already told you not to steal. God does not tell you that someone other than your spouse is your soul mate: He already told you that marriage is a promise. If you aren't familiar with God's way of life revealed in the Bible, or how it applies today, you can always ask a trusted mentor or pastor. Wise people are very helpful with discerning God's guidance. They can weigh in with their own experience and a more objective point of view. It's worth investing in relationships with mature people who care about you and who have a long track record of prayerfully listening to God themselves.

Our confidence in God's voice grows the more we listen. Sometimes clarity comes as a complete gift of grace, but we will have more certainty in God's direction the more we intentionally listen to Him every day. Especially when we don't have any agenda other than hearing whatever God has to say. If we only listen for God's voice to give us answers for specific decisions or areas of life, we'll quickly find that He doesn't work like a Magic 8-Ball. Learning to recognize God's voice isn't a search for answers; it's a process of learning who God is, what He is like, and the kinds of things He has to say. God speaks to us like a mother coos over her baby, so her child will not only know her voice but also know her love. The more we listen, the more God's words will reveal His heart to us.

At times, we long for that connection and His embrace, but instead God's guidance and presence feel more like silence, which can be painful and confusing. Silence is not proof of distance or abandonment. Silence is one of God's many voices that can direct us, and we can learn to recognize Him even in the dark.

God is not a micromanager, and although in some cases He might have very specific directions for us, in many cases He is happy for us to exercise our freedom responsibly. Like a good father, He knows that part of helping us mature is giving us more and more space to act independently. In any strong relationship, a healthy silence can indicate trust and understanding. God's silence is always for a purpose. Sometimes silence serves to bring us back to His presence when we've wandered, sometimes to allow us to grow, sometimes for us to rest in our faith, and sometimes to better enjoy the sweet embrace of a longed-for reconnection.

Silence can develop our hunger for God's voice. When He breaks His silence, He sometimes tell us things that we don't want to hear. Things like "Wait" or "No" or "Don't you see you need forgiveness too?" When we listen for God's voice, we can't listen selectively. We have to open our lives as well as our ears and allow God to speak freely as God. Even if His words are hard to hear, they are always accompanied by a "Fear not! I am with you." God will never abandon us, and there's nothing that can separate us from His love (Romans 8:38–39). Even in the silence, God is with us.

Recognizing God's voice is critically important because He isn't the only one speaking. Satan has a voice, too, and he knows how to get into our heads. He will be the first to tell us, for instance, that we are fakers, unworthy, unloved—and we may as well just give up. He has been around for ages, so he knows humans all too well. He knows our personalities and weaknesses. He knows just the right way to tempt us, cut us down, and keep us too busy, doubtful, or apathetic to pray or listen at all. He has a tone, too, that gets easier to recognize with time. He's mean, argumentative, and manipulative. He's always striking deals and explaining complicated justifications for things we know are wrong. He loves to stroke us and tell us how great we are as much as he loves to deride us and tell us how worthless we are. As long as our focus stays on ourselves, he's quite content with our pride.

I've started to recognize the lies that Satan likes to use on me. He never comes in a red cape, and he leaves his pitchfork at home. But he loves to ask me—and probably you—the same question that he asked Eve in the garden: "Did God *really* say . . . ?" (Genesis 3:1, emphasis added). He's constantly throwing doubt over the words God has spoken to us.

Satan stands over my shoulder, invisibly, as I look in the mirror. He loves to tell me I'm unworthy of love, and unfit to do what God has asked me to do. No matter how many times God whispers His love or reminds me of my purpose, I let doubt torture me. Of course, saying these things out loud makes them sound ridiculous, so I highly recommend speaking aloud the words of Satan's attacks. Say them to your praying friends, and say them to the Lord in prayer and ask Him if they are true.

> We have to open our lives as well as our ears and allow God to speak freely as God. Even if His words are hard to hear, they are always accompanied by a "Fear not! I am with you."

Your enemy's words will quickly lose their power. But realize that another and slightly tweaked attack will be coming soon. Be ready. Also realize that the enemy's words aren't always cruel; sometimes they're delicious. He loves to tell me, for instance, how right I am when I'm angry at someone, and he's quick to assist me in recalling the grudges I have against someone else. Sometimes Satan's voice is actually much more enjoyable than God's voice telling me, "That's your pride throwing a fit. Don't be so easily offended" or "Don't be bitter." The more we practice listening to God's true voice, the more obvious and menacing Satan's voice becomes. The more words of God we know, the more truth we are able to defend ourselves with. One verse that comes to mind over and over again is John 10:10, which tells us that "the thief comes only to steal and kill and destroy; I have come that they may have life, and have it to the full." When I'm trying to determine if words are from the enemy or from God, I look at where those words lead me. Are they trying to *steal* my confidence or joy, *kill* my work, or *destroy* my marriage? Those are from the enemy. Are they leading me toward a more abundant life (even if there is hard truth that needs to be faced)? Those are from God.

Not every voice in our mind comes fom God or the devil. We should be aware that our own thoughts and desires speak to us as well, and many of us carry echoes of words that other people have spoken over us. Some light, and some dark. Even our own thoughts and questions, desires, and emotions can be valuable for God to draw attention to. He will sometimes draw our attention to ourselves so that He can speak to our motives and passions. We will experience that kind of interaction more as we expect to hear Him in our everyday lives.

We won't ever get to the point where we are 100 percent sure of God's intentions 100 percent of the time. His divine wisdom and input will never be ours to control. But why are we listening anyway? We don't listen to God's voice so we can know the answers; we listen so we can know *Him*.

God's voice is recognizable by its quality, the Holy Spirit, and the content of what He says. His words lead us toward life. They lead us to Him. As we listen, self-reflection and prayer are vital elements of learning how to recognize His unique voice. We know that our enemy and our own thoughts are constantly vying for our attention. Take the time to look back at how God has led you to where you are. God is so often with us, guiding us and speaking to us without our noticing Him, that to learn His voice we need to recognize what He has already told us. God's words are often confirmed in multiple ways. When we are unsure of what He has said or whether what we heard was His voice, we can always ask Him directly. He will often get our attention another way or confirm His voice in Scripture, by circumstances, through other people, or in any of the ways we can expect to hear Him speak.

> We don't listen to God's voice so we can know the answers; we listen so we can know *Him*.

You are not on a difficult quest to hear God at the top of a foreboding mountain. God is the One pursuing you. Not only can you hear Him, but when you do, you will also understand Him. He's not being coy or speaking in riddles. His voice is speaking for your good, for your formation, and to build an authentic relationship with you. He has good words to bring you peace, wisdom, freedom, and purpose. He is writing a big beautiful story, and He has something to tell you about the part He has designed for you to play. You'll never believe the role He's designed for you. It's greater than you would ever imagine for yourself. Listen closely. God knows who He made you to be. When you learn to recognize His voice, He'll tell you things about who you are and who He is that will completely change how you experience life in this broken, beautiful world.

WHAT GOD HAS SAID,
AND WHAT HE IS SAYING

Consider taking time to process your own journey in a journal. Share with a friend who is a good listener—and listen to their story too.

1. Read John 10:24–30. When have you heard God speak to you? Why were you able to recognize His voice?

2. When, if ever, have you seen God's voice confirmed by His glory, through the Holy Spirit, or in Scripture?

3. Make a list of fifteen things you know are true about you, God, or the world based on God's voice in the Bible and your experience. Look through the list and remember the way God told you those truths. Do you see any patterns?

4. Why is hearing God's voice important to you? What do you do to listen?

CHAPTER 3

RESPONDING TO GOD'S INVITATIONS

I spent forty days of Lent disappointing God.

It started with a crash and shards of glass flying into every corner of the bathroom. A tentative voice from downstairs called up, "Everyone okay?" My favorite perfume—the one I had used through store samples of for years before I could buy an entire bottle—had slipped from my hands and hit the floor to cause a surprisingly dramatic explosion. A small crater in the tile still memorializes that morning, when the entire bathroom was overwhelmed in an instant with the fragrance of real perfume.

I held my breath and felt the tightening of my gut and diaphragm. All of the perfume was gone. The smell was so strong, I wasn't sure I even liked "tuberose and gardenia with notes of sandalwood" anymore. I grabbed paper towels and a garbage bag, trying to soak up as much of the perfume as I could before I dragged the broom across the floor. Careful to notice the smallest glimmers of glass shards, I patted and rubbed circles around the puddles on the path where bare feet walk. My hands soaked in the oils through the towels, and part of me didn't want to ever wash them again. The bottle had fallen right in front of my toes, and my feet were saturated. I washed them off in the tub. As I ran my fingers through my toes, I couldn't help but think of Mary Magdalene and the time that she broke her costly perfume bottle wide open over the feet of Jesus. I wondered if His anointed feet smelled as strong as mine, or if her hands had also taken on the scent. Days after, when a gentle breeze would remind me of how well skin absorbs perfume, I would think of Mary and Jesus.

That's when a beautiful thought turned into a bad idea.

It was almost Lent, so I decided to be like Mary and pour out my greatest sacrifices for Jesus. All of them. Not something easy like giving up chocolate, but true spiritual disciplines. A strict diet seemed to make sense. (I wouldn't mind losing a few pounds anyway.) I would also read through a devotional every day of Lent. Well, actually two devotionals. Also, I was curious about the Passover, so I announced I would be hosting my own Seder for our small group. A discipline of fasting from unhealthy foods, a discipline of reading, and a discipline of learning—I was genuinely excited to see what amazing results all of this discipline would bring to my life by Easter Sunday. It was the spiritual version of picking out my summer swimsuit on the first day of my diet.

I approached Lent committed to enriching my spiritual life through discipline, to paying attention to God through sacrifice, and to paying attention to Him by adding six books to my nightstand. But this is not actually paying attention, not true listening or *shema*. It may sound similar, but it couldn't be more different. What I thought was a discipline of listening to God was actually my own spiritual discipline of self-help.

The word for *listen* in Hebrew is *shema*. It's most famously found in Deuteronomy 6, as the first word of the *Shema* prayer: "Hear, O Israel: the LORD our God, the LORD is one" (v. 4). In *Strong's Hebrew Dictionary*, *shema* (H8085) has a fascinatingly broad definition. The primary definition is threefold: to hear, to listen, to obey. *Shema* also means to listen as an act of yielding to another. When we listen to God, we have to yield to Him by not always being the one to talk. We may need to set down our journal and pen, pause our prayer, and yield to a space of silence so that we can listen. Hear. Respond.

During one of my Lenten devotions, after I was already eight days behind in my second devotional book and had eaten Gummi Bears for dinner the night before, I encountered Jesus dining with His disciples as I read John 13. I sat with the story of the Last Supper, picturing the scene the way the many paintings and tapestries I've seen depict it. I saw Peter making his big promises to Jesus . . . and Christ without a hint of judgment telling him that he would never be able to do all of that. And my diet, devotions, Passover, and disappointments flashed before me like Peter's own zealous promises. I was overcome by Christ's love, by knowing that my expectations of myself had been marvelously different from God's expectations of me. His hopes were so wildly different for me that even though I had utterly failed at my resolutions, I had failed at things that didn't matter to God much after all.

> The promises I made for Lent were made *to* Christ, but they weren't made *for* Him. I didn't ask Him what would bring Him joy or how He would like me to celebrate His resurrection.

The promises I made for Lent were made *to* Christ, but they weren't made *for* Him.

I didn't ask Him what would bring Him joy or how He would like me to celebrate His resurrection. My promise of worship had been a pledge to prove myself: if He could suffer, I could suffer. Still, I could see in the eyes of Christ, on the verge of His death, not a shred of disappointment in me because of my broken promises or my brokenness that gave birth to those promises. I saw only love. Only forgiveness.

In a hungry effort to seize that forgiveness, I prayed. I had already changed the rules of my diet in the first week and skipped some of the devotions that didn't look interesting. Not only had I failed to keep my many Lenten promises, but I had made the wrong promises from the very beginning. It was all a pious hijacking of Christ's resurrection to be about me instead of Him. My salvation, my faith, my promises, my worship—oh, dear Jesus! Would it be possible for me to look at You for one moment with the same selfless love that You have for Peter, with the same love that You have in Your eyes when You look at me?

I returned to the Last Supper and read the passage again. This time I sat inside the passage, instead of in front of it. I could see Peter making his bold promise as though he were making it to me, and I could feel Christ's sigh of knowing. His perfectly balanced love for every part of who Peter was with His vision of who Peter would become. I realized that I was very close to Christ in my imagination of the story: instead of the apostle John, it was me who was leaning against the rough linen on Jesus's chest.

John reclined against Jesus at this same dinner where Peter declared his devotion. That was where I was invited to be. Not at the end of the table, promising to follow Jesus to my death (or through a no-carb diet), but right up against His chest. Feeling the rhythmic inhale and exhale of His breathing. Resting comfortably, leaning in closely. No self-aggrandizing promises. Simple glances, gratitude, and shared experiences. The most basic acts of love are the raw material of worship.

I dared not move . . . or blink . . . or think. I burrowed my cheek into the soft suede of the couch that I have sat on a million times before, the cushions that my kids spilled yogurt on and slept on when they were sick. I knew it was just a couch, but against my cheek it reminded me of leaning on Jesus. It was like a thin veil that connected me to the presence of heaven on the other side. The reclining ease of Jesus was strangely embraceable as I sank into the cushions.

For the rest of Lent, as my original resolutions continued to crumble, I simply rested my hand on my cheek—like a separated lover clutches a locket—and imagined a linen tunic. *I was loved. I was forgiven. I felt close to Jesus.* On Wednesday of Holy Week, I remembered that Mary had poured her perfume on Jesus. Not to impress Him or prove her loyalty and sacrifice, but because she loved Him. I could feel Jesus silencing anyone who would dare interrupt the sweetness that He shared with her in that moment. I could feel the heaviness of His impending goodbye and the fierceness of His love.

And this is the Christ who smiles at each of us from the open tomb where the stone has been rolled away: "I did what you couldn't because I love you."

Easter—in fact, the gospel itself—is entirely about what God has done for me, not the other way around. Lent was the perfect reminder that I cannot save myself, not from the allure of Gummi Bears, let alone my sins. When it comes to obeying God, I too often hijack the opportunity to do good things for Him as a form of self-improvement or to try to impress other people. In *The Great Omission*, Dallas Willard reminds us that "grace is not opposed to effort; it's opposed to earning." In our efforts to live the grace-filled lives God calls us to, aware of His presence and His voice, we shouldn't be surprised if our first attempt leads us to deep failure. It's only when we completely fail to earn grace that we are fully free to receive it.

Despite all of our efforts to hear God's voice, we never earn the right to His presence through our discipline. We already have the grace of His invitation.

I like to think of my need for intentional time with God as a spiritual invitation to deepen my relationship with Him rather than a spiritual discipline for me to keep up. Reading, praying, serving, and other disciplines become opportunities for me to encounter God and for Him to shape my character rather than a chance to prove my spirituality or to ensure I avoid consequences for not spending time with Him.

When I offered God my own holiness, my piety was far from an obedient response. Real obedience is the result of listening and responding to what God is actually asking us to do. Real listening—*shema*—is listening first, hearing with understanding, and then responding to what God has said. *Shema* listening includes the element of our response; it is impossible to listen to God's words and not be moved by them.

We respond to God's voice by what we do as well as who we are. Our response could look like love, obedience, or worship.

First, sometimes our response to God's voice is simply *love*.

From the beginning God has given us freedom of will and

freedom of choice. Why? So we could be free to love Him, not forced to obey Him. God is gently winning us over, like someone stooping low, softly speaking to a bird, "Here sweet bird, let me hear that gorgeous song of yours" (see Song of Songs 2:14). He could have created us as obedient robots, but instead He gently loves us and proves He will not abuse His power by offering the choice whether or not we want to be with Him. He is speaking tender words of kindness, hoping we might choose to be loved.

Since my earliest memory I've been doing an exhausting audition to earn any approval I could get. You'd think from all the tap dancing and jazz hands that "I love you" would be the words I most longed to hear with every fiber of my being, but they aren't. I'm strangely skeptical of anyone who loves me. I just know they'll change their mind the minute I mess up, and that ice is too thin to stand on. I would rather God—or anyone for that matter— be impressed with me than love me. My obedience to God's words has the illusion of being something I can control. His love, on the other hand, feels like a dangerous thing to need.

That's why my heart skipped a beat as my friend began her story: "I was a perfect child because I had to be . . ." I was transported back to my own childhood and the weight of perfection I carried on my shoulders. Growing up in a home with so many rules about what I could wear, whom I could be friends with, what I could read, and how my chores had to be done, I was constantly earning my place in our family and fearing the consequences of failure.

She continued: "My dad was an alcoholic. . . ."

My other "perfect" friends with "perfect" lives had moms with incredibly high standards of cleanliness and body measurements. They had rebellious siblings whom they had to balance out. They had parents who were grieving or busy working, and they lightened Mom's and Dad's burdens by proving how self-sufficient they were. They had parents who seemed to constantly be on the brink of separation, and they hoped that being the perfect child would give them a reason to stay together.

Many of us have learned to adapt to broken situations by trying to be perfect instead of simply being loved. In light of our broken experiences with love in the past, we can easily underestimate the importance of being loved by God. We can't be unique and special and interesting enough to get His love. We can't be steady and loyal and smart enough to get His love. We can't be impressive and spiritual and obedient enough to get His love. We don't have to be the perfect child, because we have the perfect—and perfectly loving—Father. As you listen for God's voice, let your first response be to receive His fiercely unconditional love.

Next, our response to God's voice may simply be *obedience.*

Jesus said, "If you love me, you will keep my commandments" (John 14:15 ESV). Do you see how love comes first? Obedience isn't our gateway to love; it's our response to God's love. Sometimes what God invites us to do isn't what we expect, but it's always what we need. After all, spiritual invitations can take all forms. They don't always have to look like journaling or Bible reading or prayer. Although the basic habits of prayer and reading Scripture keep us anchored in God's truth and presence with us, sometimes God has additional ways of inviting us to pay attention to His voice— like the time He showed Lisa the sky.

My friend Lisa sat on a bench staring at an ivy-covered wall. She had been given a simple assignment: choose a spiritual discipline to practice daily for the next sixty days.

As she stared at the ivy, the bright green tendrils seemed to be coming closer, the walls closing in. With aging parents, frustrating family dynamics, tensions at work, and distance from her adult children all clamoring for her thoughts and attention, the distractions were inescapable. The tightening of her chest could have been the walls closing to crush her. Then she heard God's voice say, "Look up."

Lisa was exhausted and emotionally raw as she slid forward on the bench and let her head fall back against it. The sky. The big, blue, open, boundless sky. The expanse seemed to hold a message from God: "You are not trapped. You are not confined. I have you. You are contained."

We don't have to be the perfect child, because we have the perfect—and perfectly loving—Father. As you listen for God's voice, let your first response be to receive His fiercely unconditional love.

As Lisa let her eyes drop to the wall, the ivy looked beautiful for the first time, and she noticed a small hole in the wall where she could see beyond it. Yes. There was life beyond the circumstances of her life right now. Everything she felt was a limitation was actually holding her in the place God had for her. The sky had called her to that conversation with God.

"Can I look at the sky each day?" she asked her instructor. "Is that enough of a discipline?"

Lisa told him the story. He reminded her, "It's not about us being disciplined; it's about responding to the invitations God has for us."

There is no hierarchy of holiness in our practices, so long as we respond to what God impresses on our hearts with obedience instead of choosing our own way that we think looks more impressive.

Finally, sometimes when God speaks, there is no better response than *worship*.

Mary, Jesus's mother, responded to the angel's message about bearing God's Son with the Magnificat (Luke 1:46–55); Miriam responded to God's victory over the Egyptians with the Song of the Sea (Exodus 15:1–18); and David responded to God's work in his life and in the nation of Israel with psalms of praise and his own music and dancing. At times God is so good, we can't help the joy that comes flooding out in response to Him.

My husband and I took the kids to a giant warehouse full of jump houses, and by some fluke we had the place all to ourselves. We ended up on a giant inflatable maze playing dodgeball with foam balls. We chased each other through the obstacles, ambushed one another, and got in giant tickle fights. I was hiding behind a pillar waiting to throw a ball at whoever walked by next when I peeked out and spied Mike with our kids. He was being so goofy. The kids were squealing, and all three of them ended up in a pile on the floor in breathless laughter. He is such a good dad. I love that he is the dad in our family.

"God," I prayed almost without thinking, "You're a good Dad. Are You ever fun?"

I tried to remember the last time I had fun with God. The last time I played with Him. The last time we laughed. And I couldn't remember anything. Maybe that was a dumb idea. God is a good Dad in lots of other ways.

Later that day, Mike took the kids on a walk so I could have the house to myself. My prayer from earlier that day came back to me. "God, were You ever fun in the Bible? Do You play? If You'd ever want to, I'd love the chance to have fun with You."

I turned my attention to my computer and put on my classical music station as I prepared to settle in to some work. My radio app said it was playing my classical music, but instead it was playing the playlist I'd made for my kids' dance party. That wasn't right. I tried to start it up again, and it again played the same dance song. This had never happened before, and it hasn't happened since, although it could have just been a coincidence (we'll talk more about that later). But since I had just prayed and asked God if He was ever fun, I took the lyrics of this happy song as His response. Yeah, He was fun! He created fun! In the only appropriate response I could imagine, I turned up the volume to dance. I didn't only dance (badly) to a cheesy song; I laughed. Hard. Now, every time I notice God's playful spirit in nature or His sense of humor in my story, I worship Him for being a good, fun Father.

As you listen, as you notice and recognize God's voice, you will have your own way to engage with His words. I can't tell you what God has to say to you, although I know it will be good. The real adventure is hearing His voice for yourself. God is not a "how-to handbook" sort of author. The definition of *shema* is the closest we get to any sort of guideline when it comes to hearing God's voice: pay attention and listen, recognize God's voice with understanding, and respond to the words He has for you. As you listen, you'll have your very own stories of your very own encounters with God, the way you experience His presence, and your natural response to His words—I can't wait to hear them.

God has already spoken: "I am with you" (Matthew 28:20). How will you respond?

RESPONDING
TO GOD'S VOICE

Consider taking time to process your own journey in a journal. Share with a friend who is a good listener—and listen to their story too.

1. Read James 1:22–25. When, if ever, have you heard God's voice and ignored it?

2. When, if ever, have you made big promises to God— and were they for God or for you to prove yourself? What happened when you tried to keep those promises?

3. When, if ever, have you been intentional about a spiritual practice? What discipline did you choose? What was that experience like for you?

4. Is God speaking to you now? What might it look like to respond to something He is saying to you?

PART TWO

EXPECTANT
TO HEAR

CHAPTER 4

A VOICE THAT SPEAKS IN SCRIPTURE

Did you know that when cod is shipped to the United States, it is shipped alive to keep it fresh? For the fish to be at its best, it should keep swimming the entire trip. Seasick fish don't love swimming around in small circles in shipping containers, so an inventive fisherman came up with a solution to keep those fish moving. As a natural predator of cod, a catfish raises the excitement level if it is released into the shipping tank. (I kinda want to make teeny tank tops for the cod that say, "I only swim if a catfish is chasing me.")

Based on this predatory behavior, the Merriam-Webster dictionary added an additional definition for *catfish* in 2014: "Catfish" now also refers to "a person who sets up a false personal profile on a social networking site for fraudulent or deceptive purposes."

Emma Perrier, a French barista living in London, fell in love with one such predatory internet catfish. The internet predator was a balding divorcé in his fifties who lacked the confidence to engage with women in real life. He had stolen photos of a Turkish model and used them to populate his profiles. He used a fake name and wrapped Emma up in his game for an entire year, emotionally manipulating her and lying about every aspect of his identity.

With the help and support of family and friends, however, Emma finally put the pieces together. She used software to track down the original source of those photos and found the actual Turkish model they belonged to: Adem Guzel. Emma sent him a quick note on Facebook notifying him that his identity was being stolen. Although Adem initially glanced at her message and ignored it, something made him take a second look. He reached out to her, and soon they were talking and video calling. The conversation slowly shifted from Emma's dating trauma to the easy banter of a new relationship.

> I was surprised when I started to read the Bible without commentary and interpretation by my church. The Bible was even better—more real and more engaging— than the words I thought I knew.

After phone calls, video calls, and hours of conversation, Emma had to try to forget everything she thought she knew about Adem's face and get to know the real Adem. Over time, they fell for each other—for the *real* each other—and Adem moved from Turkey to London. Their love story took the Brits by storm. Emma went from loving the picture of Adem to being much more deeply in love with the man of her dreams, the really real Adem.

My love affair with the Bible is a bit of a catfishing story too. The church in which I grew up prided itself on being more biblical than anyone else. Daily Bible reading, study, and Scripture memorization were expected. We lived our lives being true to "what the Bible says" even when—maybe especially when—it was incredibly different from the way anyone else lived. The Bible had the attractive trait of being God's perfect words, but in my church those words were animated by men who wanted power and loyalty. Those men quoted Scripture to justify women wearing veils in public and being mistreated by their husbands in private. They quoted Scripture to justify large men coming in the night to kidnap a teenage boy and enlist him in reforming camp. They quoted Scripture to solicit money for the church's special projects that never happened. Even the devil quotes Scripture (Matthew 4:6).

I had the same urge Emma did when she first messaged Adem: I wanted to tell God that someone was using His name and face to fool people.

Just as Emma was surprised that her Turkish model in a black leather jacket was real and quite charming, I was surprised when I started to read the Bible without commentary and interpretation by my church. The Bible was even better—more real and more engaging—than the words I thought I knew. God's words in the Bible are fantastically beautiful. They had been seriously misrepresented to me for a long time.

My story may sound extreme, but most of us have been catfished by the Bible whether we realize it or not. It is much more common that the Bible is misrepresented as a rule book, a get-outta-hell-free manual, or a collection of inspirational quotes. The problem with these seemingly harmless representations of God's Word is that they fall far short of the way God intends for His Word to speak to us.

First of all, the Bible is all one single story, told in a mosaic of genres, describing human rebellion and God's ultimate rescue in Jesus. The story has massive implications for how we understand our world, our purpose in life, the meaning of suffering, and the way we live. Taken out of context, parts of the story distort God's voice and are easily misunderstood or misrepresented. Although every passage of Scripture is significant to the story, many of them are not meant to be applied directly to our daily lives.

I visited Monticello one fall with a friend who had lived in that area for a few years. Thomas Jefferson's estate was smaller than I imagined, but absolutely dreamy in the golden light of autumn with leaves hanging from branches and lining the edges of walkways. On our tour, we got to see where Jefferson lived, watch some of his inventions work, read letters he had written, and hear stories of his bravery. We also struggled to reconcile the grand main house with the slave quarters in the back that we had to crouch down to enter. We clearly saw contradictions in the ways Jefferson's family, friends, slaves, and political enemies recounted his life, yet every part served the greater story. Every artifact, witness, and record had a unique slant and perspective that represented a point of time in Jefferson's personal evolution. No artifact, witness, or record could tell the whole story, but together they told a much more robust story. For hours during our drive home, my friend and I talked excitedly about justice, human rights, revolution, friendship, and freedom.

The Bible is also a collection of accounts and letters and history that each hold a piece of God's story, which is not fundamentally about us nor written directly to us. The original audience had a very different worldview and was rooted in a historical context we try our best to piece together. It is raw and honest and full of paradox, more a collection of diverse literature than a history book or self-help manual. Reading a small section of the story at a time and trying to draw a practical life application from that set of words is like holding up Thomas Jefferson's quill pen and asking, "What does this say about me?"

Meant to be an immersive story that we step into, the Bible is constantly using literary clues to hook us into its themes and help us recognize its foreshadowing. It can be very difficult to understand any one part of the Bible on its own—or to understand any one part only in its relationship to our experiences. The words of Scripture may not be a story about us, but they tell a story we are invited into. Although the words were written in a different time, when we understand how to read their original intent for their original audience, we find that God's words are fresh and relevant for us today. If we want to step into the story God has for us now and hear His voice calling us from the sunset, the Bible is where we learn to recognize His words and His ways in the stories He has already told us.

No wonder the Bible is the most read, most printed, and most influential book in all human history. The content is uniquely special, a sacred collaboration between God and humans. Humans gathered and told stories. Some wrote poems, prayers, historical accounts, and letters that shared the words they heard from God. Although portions of Scripture were dictated word for word by God, He also gave humans the talent and wisdom to write the Bible in partnership with Him. They faithfully obeyed God's calling to partner as prophet, priest, scribe, or witness. The Bible may not be a scroll dropped from heaven, but it's not simply a Jewish history book either. It's written by God and humans together, and each writer's faithful work was guided by God's powerful Spirit of truth.

And this amazing Book has never been more accessible than it is in the twenty-first century. A 2013 survey determined that the average American household has more than four Bibles, most of which are never read. Like deciding sleep isn't important during finals week or breakfast isn't necessary when there's black coffee at the office, we so easily convince ourselves that we don't need God's words. After all, we've tested the limits—of sleep, breakfast, and biblical understanding—and survived enough times that we are confident about our shortcuts. When we don't read our Bibles, we sometimes feel guilty, but we rarely feel hungry.

You might remember a time when you read the Bible for a day, a week, or longer only to feel that it didn't live up to the promise to change your life or transform your connection to God. It's easy to talk about how life-changing the words of God are, but they can feel dry, confusing, or unrewarding when we actually read them. I have to wake up to my alarm and walk past the pile of dishes that need to be washed and sit in the stillness of my living room knowing that whether or not I *think* I need water or sleep or time with God, I do. Getting through some of those mornings is still hard for me, but there are a few things that help a lot.

First, I tell myself I can't bail in the first twenty minutes. If I can get twenty minutes into my time in Scripture, I'm usually forgetting why I didn't think I could wake up. Second, I start with prayer and am totally honest about how I am coming to meet God and how focused or unfocused I am. Sometimes it feels good to get it off my chest, and sometimes it is therapeutic to hear how ridiculous I sound. Last, I try to read Scripture in different ways to mix things up.

Meditation, dedication, and contemplation are three of my favorite approaches to connecting with God's story through His words. As we listen for God's voice, we shouldn't be surprised that we can learn to hear Him clearly in His own words.

First, I hear God's voice more clearly when I read the Bible practicing *meditation.*

For God's voice to sink into our minds and hearts, His words have to be there frequently, and they have to stay awhile. That's one reason the Bible tells us to meditate on the words of God. Eastern meditation is characterized by clearing your mind, but Christian meditation is about filling our mind with the words, thoughts, and images of Scripture.

When I most need to remind myself of something God has told me, I like to memorize a verse about that truth. Memorizing Scripture keeps the words fresh in my mind as I am learning them, and then when the words are in my memory they can come to mind at just the right moment. Having God's words from Scripture posted around my house or as the lock screen on my phone and repeating them many times over helps me remember what God said. Not only as words of truth, but as truth for my life as I go through my day. Once those words are in my memory, it is amazing to me the way the Holy Spirit can bring them to mind when I need them most.

For instance, 1 Corinthians 10:13 is a verse I'm glad I have memorized. It says that temptation will always be a part of our lives, but God is faithful: no matter what we are tempted with, He will always provide a way of escape. Whenever I'm lucky enough to realize that the thing I'm tempted to buy, to drink, to say, or to watch is not my best choice, I think of 1 Corinthians 10:13. Instead of finding a way to justify my bad choice, I can immediately look for the escape route. It's always there.

I might spend a whole week thinking about a single verse, but it's not the quantity of God's words we consume that matters; it's the quality of our engagement with them. Some days when I am reading through a section of Scripture, a single verse will seem to jump off the page. When it does, I let it stop me in my tracks and repeat it over and over out loud or write it out in fancy letters in my journal. I'll think about each word.

I spent months in Psalm 34 a few years ago. There was so much to pay attention to even in verse 4: "I sought the LORD, and he answered me; he delivered me from all my fears." I wrote it over and over in my journal, focusing on a new word each time.

> "I sought the LORD, and he answered me; he delivered me
> from all my *fears*."
> What am I afraid of right now? (This was an easy—
> and long—list to make.)
> "I *sought* the LORD, and he answered me; he delivered me
> from all my fears."
> What am I doing to seek God? What could I or should I
> be doing to seek God? Why is He the last One I run to
> instead of the first?
> "I sought the LORD, and he *answered* me; he delivered me
> from all my fears."
> In what ways does God answer me? When and how has
> He answered me in the past? What am I doing to listen
> for Him to speak to me now? Am I expecting Him to
> answer when I seek Him?

"I sought the LORD, and he answered me; he *delivered* me
from all my fears."

What does deliverance look like? Will I ever escape my
nightmares? What does it feel like to not be afraid? In
what ways would my life change if I wasn't so afraid of
being abandoned?

"I sought the LORD, and he answered me; he delivered me
from all my fears."

Who do I go to with all my fears? Who am I expecting to
answer me and deliver me? How does being "Lord"
help me understand what God is like?

I could have read all of Psalm 34 easily in a morning, but this
one verse took up three or four days in my journal. It might seem
crazy to spend so much time on one single verse, but if we race past
the words God has for us, we will never fully hear all He has to say.

There is no shortcut in meditation. You can't just find the most
popular verses in the Bible and choose one to sit with. Most often
this kind of study focuses on a verse I couldn't have predicted. A
verse or phrase or even a single word surprises me when I'm doing
something else, and I allow myself to be captured by it instead of
rushing past it. It's that simple. When you are listening for God in
His Word, let Him get your attention, sidetrack you, surprise you.
Chase rabbit holes and get curious about where else in the Bible
that phrase shows up or what the context of that Old Testament
quote is.

Meditating on God's words helps us not to rush through and
miss the fun of spending time with God. I like to think of my time
with God as an opportunity to enjoy His company. Just like in any

of my relationships, I need to really slow down to make that connection. To allow His words to really move through my mind, to engage my thoughts and emotions, to connect to my actual fears and desires. The Bible talks about us meditating day and night. Meditating on Scripture can help us start our day focused on God and His possibility and then end our day with a heart of gratitude and reassurance about the faithfulness of God.

In addition to *meditation,* I hear God's voice more clearly when I read the Bible with *dedication.*

Having a set routine can help me continue to connect with God even on days I'm tired, lazy, or not feeling aware of His presence. The best way to read the Bible is to interact with it as often as you can. The Bible has its own language and nuances, not just in the translation that you use but also in the way the different genres read or in the literary devices that are utilized. The more you read the Bible, the more familiar you become with its themes, symbols, and structure. The Bible becomes easier to understand and more interesting to read.

"Did someone just die?" my husband asked.

"Actually, honey, three people just died."

Every summer, simply because he loves me, Mike eats a picnic with me at the free Shakespeare in the Park near our city. I fell in love with Shakespeare in junior high. The language is odd, and a lot of the jokes are funnier if you understand the culture they were written for. Since I've been reading, watching, and studying Shakespeare for over a decade, I had almost forgotten how foreign it could sound to someone hearing it for the first or even the tenth time.

Similarly, it takes some adjusting to get over the initial language and style of Scripture. Once you do, you'll discover you are reading some of the best satire, drama, comedy, and romance ever written. The characters and stories will capture your imagination. Like good art, the Bible makes us think and puts forward questions we are invited to wrestle with. If you're new to the Bible, don't be discouraged if it seems confusing or boring. You're reading an ancient book, and it takes some mental adjustment and effort.

The Bible talks about us meditating day and night. Meditating on Scripture can help us start our day focused on God and His possibility and then end our day with a heart of gratitude and reassurance about the faithfulness of God.

I still hear Jesus whisper, "You don't know Me," and His mystery pulls me in. I have a voracious curiosity. If life had its own high school yearbook, I might be voted "Most Likely to Ask Questions." When I approach God's words and something catches my attention, I love to study and research that word or passage so I can grasp what God might have to teach me. Dedicated and focused attention will lead us to the truth God has for us when we read the Bible, lean in, and say, "Tell me more." Commentaries and original language tools aren't just for nerds. They are tools to help us dig and discover deeper meaning. I love using free online Bible study tools like Lumina, and I'm so thankful for access to so many sermons, podcasts, and blogs from trusted sources.

Bible reading plans have also been really helpful for me. They give me a set period of time and a goal to keep me accountable. I love finding a good plan and doing it with friends so we can cheer each other on. Reading plans can last anywhere from five days to a year, and you can always start small. You can always make up your own plan by choosing a book of the Bible and reading a chapter a day. Reading Matthew, Mark, Luke, or John gives us the best chance to hear God's voice through the words of Jesus. James is five chapters long and makes a great Monday through Friday one-week reading plan. The book of Proverbs has thirty-one chapters, and that's a chapter a day for most months. My favorite plan for reading the Bible in a year is called Read Scripture. It's free and has lots of context information and short, helpful videos provided by the Bible Project at TheBibleProject.com.

At whatever pace you decide to read the Bible, try using a journal to keep track of what questions you have, ideas that come to mind, and how your understanding of God and yourself is being stretched. Even if you don't meet your goal or you miss a day or a week of reading, don't be discouraged. The real goal is to keep going. Don't give up. When you dedicate yourself to reading the Bible consistently over time, you might see changes in your attitude, lifestyle, and relationships that surprise you. God's words will change us.

As important as I know dedication to God's Word is, it does not come easily to me. I'm more of a starter than a finisher. Desperation was truly the only reason I persevered in one of my reading plans. When I was thirty years old, I had my first experience with depression after my son was born. He was healthy and I loved him, but I felt like a bad mom because I wasn't happy and didn't totally know why. I tried to explain it to my husband, but I felt like a bad wife because he didn't know why I wasn't happy either. I tried to read my Bible and pray, but the words had lost their spark. I didn't find the comfort there that had encouraged me in the past.

I felt like a bad Christian because I couldn't be happy, and my faith wasn't big enough to fix me.

What happened next still surprises me.

Two friends and I decided to read the entire Bible in ninety days. It was an intense reading plan that we were all drawn to for different reasons, but we all stuck to the program and finished together. It was incredible! At the time I was the mother of a nineteen-month-old and a three-month-old. I didn't shower most days, I wore my pajama pants to the grocery store, and I was running on empty. My oldest still liked to be held and was jealous of the baby, so I literally had a baby on each hip and looked like a cartoon of a worn-down mom. It was not the time to be training for a marathon or reading the Bible for an hour every day, but then again it was actually the perfect time. I would wake up in the cold darkness before dawn and sit in the quiet of my living room, alone for the only time I would have to myself all day. I had a soft blanket, a cup of coffee, and my Bible, and it was so much better than sleep. In fact, it was the time of day I felt most awake.

The three of us met at a coffee shop every Friday to talk about what we had read during the week. We were the crazy but smiling ones standing out in the dark, shivering in the cold, knocking gently on the glass door, beckoning our barista to open the shop on time. After a few weeks she started letting us in early.

God didn't just speak to me through His words in the Bible. He also spoke to me through the words He gave my friends. The things that they noticed and their unique experiences made the Bible come alive to me in a fresh and exciting way. When God speaks to us and we share His words with one another, we all remember to expect His voice and trust His nearness. At times we would read Scripture aloud to each other like the early Christians did. Hearing the words of God from others and in a group setting was an incredible reminder that these words of God are for me, but they aren't only for me. They're for all of us.

Reading giant chunks of Scripture offers a unique perspective. You realize who is related to whom, and the stories are more connected. Themes and repetition become more obvious. I knew that the story of Pharaoh and the plagues and God's rescue of Egypt was in Exodus, but I had no idea that it was retold and referenced dozens of times in the rest of the Bible.

When I started reading, I just wanted my joy back. I didn't know if there was a verse that could fix me. I was frustrated that God felt distant and the Bible had lost its potency right when I needed both of them the most. And, if I'm honest, part of me wanted to prove that the problem wasn't on my end.

I didn't find a magic verse, but that wasn't what I actually needed. Instead, I needed to see God's kindness and faithfulness play out thousands of times over thousands of years. I needed to anchor myself in the hope that His faithfulness and kindness are still inescapable now.

I needed to see Jacob wrestle with God, wrestling despite his exhaustion, grappling through the night, and refusing to let go until God blessed him. I found my own sacred struggling ground of grace. "Wrestle with Me," God said. I had spent too much of my energy wrestling with my demons of depression on my own. I needed to wrestle with God instead.

It wasn't that I was a bad mom, wife, or Christian. I was simply a woman who needed help. I needed to let go of the shame of not being happy and grab on to God fiercely, with the dogged strength of Jacob, believing He had a way of joy and purpose for me. As Frederick Buechner preached in *The Magnificent Defeat*, "Power, success, happiness, as the world knows them, are his who will fight for them hard enough; but peace, love, joy, are only from God." I finally heard God's invitation to receive joy from Him instead of insisting I could defeat depression on my own. He led me gently to the right friends and referrals so I could learn to be weak, learn to be dependent, and learn to ask for the help that I had needed for a long time.

The initial drudgery of my Bible reading gave way to a natural rhythm. It took some time, but I started to look forward to my daily reading as a treat. I came to God's Word looking for wisdom and inspiration, and I was utterly astonished by the way He met me in those early hours with His actual company. His words taught me perspective, but the steadfast love—the loyal and unending love of God that the Bible refers to hundreds of times—didn't stay on the page. It washed over me and through me like a waterfall of acceptance, belonging, and being known. In those deep, rushing waters, I started to learn that I was seen, loved, and eternally important. God's Word told me so.

In addition to *meditation* and *dedication*, I hear God's voice more clearly when I read the Bible with *contemplation*.

God's words will flow off the page and wrap us in His goodness when we give them the space and attention they need. They are the starting point of a two-way conversation.

You see, the Holy Spirit inspired men and women to tell the history of God's people and His plan of redemption in the Scriptures, and that same Spirit is inside of us. When we read Scripture, the same Spirit who knows the perfect intent of His own words is actively working in us to teach us the ways of God and help us move closer to Him. The Holy Spirit is a beautiful gift from God, and to try to read the Scripture exclusively from our own intellect and strength without Him will leave our experience with the Bible well below its divine potential.

Interestingly, throughout church history, Catholics, Protestants, and Puritans have all used basically the same approach to read the Bible deeply and in conversation with God. It has been called divine reading, *Lectio Divina*, or spiritual reading. Honoring the overlap and commonality of these diverse traditions, we can call it *contemplative reading*. The process looks something like this:

a. Prepare yourself to read.

b. Read the Scripture slowly and do so multiple times.

c. Let the Holy Spirit draw your attention to a word or phrase.

d. Pray about what you have read, asking the Holy Spirit to make its message personal.

e. Leave space to listen for God's response.

Before beginning contemplative reading, prepare your space and your mind to be still and focused. I like to light a candle and watch the flame for a moment or two. I know it's not a burning bush and God is not in the fire, but the candle helps me focus and reminds me that I am setting this time and space aside to meet with God.

When I am doing contemplative reading, I try to take a small enough section of verses that I can read slowly and multiple times. Sometimes I will choose a Bible translation that I don't normally read just to keep my mind from racing ahead in familiar passages.

Coming to the Bible is like walking on a familiar path, but even those familiar spaces have fresh surprises every time I return. That's one reason I like to make reading the stories of Jesus in the Gospels a regular part of my time in Scripture. I recently reread a journal entry I wrote just over two years ago after reading the story of Jesus and the rich young ruler in Mark 10:17–31.

After reading that story slowly a few times, I took the chance to expand the passage. I asked the Holy Spirit to draw my attention to what He would have me notice. With the help of the Holy Spirit and using the beautiful gift of imagination that God has given us, I entered into the story as best I could. Instead of looking at the characters as if they were illustrations in a book, I stood among them and stared into their faces. I tried to feel the tension of the problem at hand—the anxiety, pain, or joy of the moment—as best I could relate to it. I didn't believe for a moment that I was actually entering into the historical reconstruction of the story. Just as we have children dress up like pioneers and take a turn at the butter churn to make history come alive, I remembered that the Bible tells stories of real events and real people. By inviting my imagination to the story and staying as close as I could to the text, I was open to any fresh words the Holy Spirit had for me.

> The Holy Spirit is a beautiful gift from God, and to try to read the Scripture exclusively from our own intellect and strength without Him will leave our experience with the Bible well below its divine potential.

Sometimes words come from the story, and sometimes the Spirit speaks to me about why I am imagining things. Why, for instance, am I projecting that motive on this person, or what is it about another person that attracts me so intensely? Sometimes a popular or powerful verse stands out in a text, but when I wait inside a story, the Spirit might have words specifically for me.

In the story of the rich young ruler, a man came to follow Jesus but changed his mind when Jesus said that to follow Him, this man would need to sell all that he owned and abandon his wealth and status. This story has always prompted me to ask myself what comfort or security or wealth I am more devoted to than Jesus. This time in my reading, however, as I stood beside the young ruler, the Spirit immediately drew my attention to verse 21 instead.

The rich and religious young man had just told Jesus that he had kept every commandment from his youth. I immediately raised my eyebrows and wanted to roll my eyes so Jesus could see I am in on this joke. The man's overconfidence and self-righteousness are obviously ridiculous. No one has been perfect since childhood. My judgment can't bristle for long, though. This rich young ruler and I are too similar. I wrote in my journal:

> I am like this ruler. . . . I grew up trying to obey God and missing the point. . . . I kept the rules (more or less) as a "good Christian girl" from childhood but didn't love others well and have always chased money for security, independence, and affirmation.

Instead of calling this young man out on his obvious hypocrisy, "Jesus, looked at him and loved him" (v. 21).

In exploring this passage, I asked the Holy Spirit to help me sense Christ's heart for this young man. Instead of asking how I could be less attached to my money, I wanted to know how to stand before Christ as a foolish hypocrite and still feel loved by Him. I wanted to imagine the softness of His face and the tenderness in His eyes that spoke love. I wrote in my journal that I tried to concentrate and enter into the love of Christ, to let Him look on me as well as the ruler with love. My handwriting is scrawled: "I am very tired, and it's hard to concentrate. I will try again later."

It's hard to focus, to enter the stories of Scripture with the Spirit as your guide. After I have read and expanded a section of Scripture, I spend time in prayer. After my encounter with the young ruler, I thanked God for drawing my attention to the love of Christ and told Him I would love a deeper experience of it. I developed a longing to know the tenderness of Jesus's love, and even though it didn't happen at that moment, I let the desire sit unsatisfied so that the Holy Spirit could grow it inside me. Grace is worth anticipating. When I pray after reading, I have an opportunity to voice my gratitude, wants, needs, and frustrations to God. I remember that the Holy Spirit is with me and translates my prayers even when I have no words (Romans 8:26).

After I pray, I sit in silence to listen for God's response. Sometimes those moments seem quite silent. Other times I'll be a little annoyed that I want to talk to God about something specific and instead He brings to mind someone I need to forgive or a wrong attitude I need to confess. God isn't our ventriloquist dummy: we don't get to speak for Him or interact with Him on our terms. Asking the Holy Spirit to help us enter a conversation with God, we have to desire most of all His company, not what feelings

He can give us or what answers He might have to our pressing questions. After all, silence can be the sound of two people who are happy simply being together.

Months after my reading of the young ruler passage, my Lenten reading of John caught me by surprise when I had an overwhelming feeling of Christ's love as, after the resurrection, He forgave Peter for denying Him. The way I felt His loving redemption was a sweet and unexpected gift from the Holy Spirit. And something I almost forgot I had prayed for. The love of Christ is unchanged by my sense of His nearness or distance, and sometimes my heart needs to be prepared to receive it. I need to leave space for God to answer me; I need to sit with Him in silence and believe He is near even when He is unseen. We may not always hear His voice clearly or right away, yet in the dark silence His whispers are most easily heard. I have learned not to be afraid of spending time there.

Finally, God's voice speaks to me through Scripture for my *transformation.*

Meditation, dedication, and contemplation are just three of many pathways to encounter Scripture. Ultimately the goal is transformation: to be more like Jesus. When we spend the time to linger in Scripture, the hope is that God's words will reshape our thoughts and character and purpose.

In 2 Peter 3:14–18, Peter ended his farewell letter to the churches of Asia Minor by encouraging them to continue to learn the wisdom of God found in the apostle Paul's letters (the letters that make up a good part of the New Testament). In 2 Peter 3:16, Peter acknowledged that "there are some things in [the letters] that are hard to understand, which the ignorant and unstable twist to their own destruction" (ESV). It's comforting to me when I hear that I'm not the only one who thinks that the Bible is hard to understand. Even the apostle Peter acknowledged it can be difficult. The early church and God Himself knew all too well the ways the Bible would be twisted and manipulated by the ignorant and self-deceived catfishes out there. Still, Peter encouraged us to press through the parts of Scripture that are confusing, to push aside the ways the Bible has been manipulated, and instead to "grow in the grace and knowledge of our Lord and Savior Jesus Christ" (v. 18). God's Word still speaks to us today, teaching us who God is and how to live our lives in the freedom for which we were made.

> Ultimately the goal is transformation: to be more like Jesus. When we spend the time to linger in Scripture, the hope is that God's words will reshape our thoughts and character and purpose.

God's voice isn't just one of comfort. His words will change us forever. He loves us too much to let us stay the same. Our image of Him may be hazy or broken, but His imagination for how He can restore the ashes of our world is limitless. That story of redemption is the story the Bible sweeps us into. And nothing could be more worthy of our time and imagination.

HEARING GOD'S VOICE
IN SCRIPTURE

Read through these invitations to hear God speak through Scripture. Which practice might help you listen for God's voice?

1. Choose a reading plan that you can stick to and that feels easy to finish. Invite a friend to join you.

2. Choose a verse from Scripture that caught your attention during your reading plan. Read it every morning and every evening this week. Consider making it the wallpaper for your cell phone or computer. Make an effort to memorize it by the end of the week.

3. Try contemplative reading. Slow down and take a fresh look at the experience of Scripture. Choose a passage from Matthew, Mark, Luke, or John that tells a story with Jesus as a main character. Then do the following:

   a. Prepare yourself to read.
   b. Read the Scripture slowly several times.
   c. Let the Holy Spirit draw your attention to a word or phrase.
   d. Pray about what you have read, asking the Holy Spirit to make its meaning personal.
   e. Leave space to listen for God's response.

CHAPTER 5

A VOICE THAT SPEAKS IN PRAYER

I opened my first e-mail from the prayer team, completely unprepared for what I would find.

A few days earlier I'd had a surge of ambition when our pastor said the team needed help. I believe prayer is powerful, it changes things, and it changes me. I also think prayer is part of being in community, and we all should be praying for each other. So of course I would help the prayer team. I had confidently—and a tad idealistically—scrawled my name and e-mail address on the response card.

On Wednesday, the prayer team e-mail came. It was not an enthusiastic note of thanks for my new membership. It was an unceremonious spreadsheet with 237 prayer requests on it.

Even if I only spent a minute praying for each one, I'd be praying for almost four hours. With two young kiddos and the demands of beginning a new study program, I decided now was not my time to be on the prayer team. Maybe when I am retired? I could definitely see myself having a weekly prayer brunch when

I'm old and don't have a million other things to do. I'm really good at making scones, and if I am feeling sassy in my seventies, I could set down a tray of mimosas in my living room and watch the white-haired ladies blush.

With that plan in mind, I contacted the prayer team to respectfully resign or at least postpone my membership for a couple of decades. A college student, who was busier than I was, replied to my e-mail with so much kindness and easy freedom that I was a little embarrassed by her simple idea. She would happily take me off the e-mail list, but would I consider staying on and just praying for even one person a day?

Oh, uh . . . sure. I can do that.

I can be so all-or-nothing with prayer. I think I have to be in full monastic mode or praying for hours on end to do it "right," and that makes me want to quit before I start. I wonder if I sat in the lotus position on a platform overlooking the ocean, complete calm on my face, for thirty days in a row, if I would finally feel like a prayer warrior. For now, my prayer life is more like peanut butter ChapStick.

"I don't need ChapStick," my son once explained to me.

"Come on, sweetie. Your lips are red and cracked. ChapStick will help you feel better."

"No, Mom. I just keep a little peanut butter on my lips after I eat my toast. Then later I can smear it around with my tongue— and it tastes a lot better than ChapStick."

I truly love spending time with God, but I don't pray with enough discipline. I also wish I could pray longer and be less distracted when I do. My prayer life works for me, but I'm not sure I'm always doing it the best way. For all my scattered ineptitude, my conversations with God are still meaningful, still sweet. I don't have to be a great talker. God is kind enough to carry the conversation even when I am awkward or shy. All I have to do is show up. There are a few things that I've learned make it easier for me to be present with God when I pray.

First, I am most present when I pray both spontaneously *and* by appointment.

I think about my husband and me and all the rich conversations we've had when we've scheduled a time and intentionally invested in one another. Yet my heart races when there are unexpected flowers on the counter or when he surprises me with soft kisses on my neck while I'm making dinner. Spontaneous moments are an overflow of the heart, and the scheduled moments help keep our hearts in the right place. If Mike and I didn't have any scheduled time together— if we never looked ahead at our calendar and made sure connection time was part of the craziness—those spontaneous moments wouldn't happen.

Spontaneous prayer is an important part of my day. I let my heart overflow when I'm feeling thankful, or I notice beauty and easily slip into worship. I also let my heart spill over when I'm feeling stressed or insecure, and I take those feelings to God as well. The more present I am with my own thoughts and emotions, the easier it is for me to be present with God. Nothing kills my prayer life faster than running

> For all my scattered ineptitude, my conversations with God are still meaningful, still sweet. I don't have to be a great talker. God is kind enough to carry the conversation. . . . All I have to do is show up.

from what I'm feeling or numbing myself with TV, social media, or shopping.

Spontaneous prayer wouldn't flow from my lips if I didn't have time with God intentionally set aside. I've tried a few different rhythms, but right now I go with a first-word/last-word approach. The first word or thought when I wake up is a prayer for the day ahead. The last word or thought of the night is a prayer from the day that has ended. This planned time frames my day in a way that helps me pay attention to God's presence with me, and it lays the foundation for plenty of spontaneous interactions in between.

I am also most present when I pray quietly *and* aloud.

For a long time I only prayed out loud when I was in a group setting. I grew up around prayer meetings, so I know how to read the breathing and the silence. I usually thought about what I was going to say before I said it, often planning the whole prayer instead of listening to the person who was praying right before I jumped in.

I only recently discovered that praying out loud helps me even when I am praying alone. Once I got over the strangeness of talking out loud to myself, I noticed two things. First, thinking of words and then having them come out of my mouth and then back into my ears gave me more connection points with my own words. I started to notice, for instance, the pronouns I used or the way I said things and the words I chose. I then paid more attention to my prayers and noticed my own physical posture more quickly. Next, praying aloud really helped me stay focused and not have my thoughts go trailing off. I can be praying silently in my thoughts and not notice for several minutes that I have begun fantasizing about taking a vacation, but when I pray out loud, the momentum of my speech keeps me present in my prayer.

Next, I am most present when I pray with my mind *and* body. Bible teacher Beth Moore lined the stage with props, including boots and a chair, as she got ready to teach about prayer. "Face, knees, seat, feet"—she had us say this over and over. She had done a study through Scripture of the different body postures people had when they prayed as well as what types of prayers they tended to pray in each posture. I found my notes to double-check, and even though my journal is four years old, I had the words right the first time I typed them: *face, knees, seat, feet.*

Over the past four years, I've tried to notice my physical posture when I pray. Research shows that our body language doesn't only communicate how we are feeling, but it also affects how we are feeling. Confident people tend to have a more confident posture (they take up more space with their arms or legs). More surprisingly, even people who are nervous tend to feel more self-assured when they practice a confident body posture. Our posture both communicates and shapes our thoughts, so it can be helpful to consider the positions of our bodies as we pray.

When I am keenly aware of God's nearness or of my own desperate need for forgiveness, I lie on the ground, forehead to the floor.

When I am pleading with the Lord, knocked over in wonder of Him, or committing myself to obey, I pray on my knees.

When I am praying in polite company or with confidence, I pray sitting down.

When I am praying with focus and attention, I pray standing up.

Face, knees, seat, feet. Our bodies can help us pray.

Once I was home alone listening to worship music while I was cleaning. Praying as I worked, I was suddenly aware of God's love. A song began to play in the background, an old hymn that captured the moment perfectly, and my prayer unexpectedly changed from words to the movement of a dance. Even though I'm not a dancer, I was able to express through movement the fears and happiness I was struggling to express through words and tears. Our bodies are invited to prayer.

I have also found I am most present when I pray alone *and* with others.

My default approach to prayer is private and alone, my prayers only living as thoughts in my head. While prayer is a conversation between God and me—and there are many times it makes sense for prayer to be private—prayer has always had a communal aspect in Christian tradition. In the New Testament we see the church praying together and for one another every time they come together.

For two years I woke up at 5:30 in the morning every Tuesday, while it was still quite dark, to curl up on the couch with my blanket and my cell phone. My friends Dawn and Tasha also had young kids and jobs, and our morning times were jam-packed from the minute the first little eyelids opened. So we carved out the only time we had, in the quiet space before the sun came up, to pray together.

When we started our Tuesday morning prayer time, we didn't know that all three of us would move within two years or that Dawn would move out of state. As we prayed through our big decisions together, big things happened. All the worries we had buzzing in our brains became prayers. We watched God guide us, surprise us, and answer our prayers in different ways. Seeing God work clearly in one another's lives made it easier to notice His presence in our own. We would see some prayers answered before the next phone call, and some were answered weeks or years later. We would remind each other, "We prayed for that!"

Praying with others—sharing the true pain and longings of our heart—will help us see God. We'll see Him answer quickly or not very quickly, obviously, or subtly. When we pray through the long waiting of some requests and the sweet celebration of others, we remember that a "no" right now may simply be a "not yet." We learn not to fear the valleys in our own lives because we have already walked through the shadows with one another. Our own experiences of God and life are just a drop in the ocean, but prayer is a way we can join in the experience of others. A way we can be as connected as water to the words and ways of God.

> When we pray through the long waiting of some requests and the sweet celebration of others, we remember that a "no" right now may simply be a "not yet." We learn not to fear the valleys in our own lives because we have already walked through the shadows with one another.

My time praying with Tasha and Dawn connected me so closely to them that we found ourselves texting one another and praying for each other constantly. Whenever my alert sounded, Mike mumbled under his breath, "I wonder who that is."

One night he surprised me when he said, "Tasha and Dawn know more about you than I do."

"Honey, c'mon. You're busy all day at work. You don't want me texting you during your meetings to tell you what I had for lunch."

"Maybe I do sometimes."

I knew that the intimacy with my prayer group was meeting

my need for connection. I was less lonely than I had been in a long time. But I had never thought of intimacy with my girlfriends as a threat to my husband. I thought it might be a gift to him if I were less needy and not pouncing on him with news about my day as he walked in the door. It wasn't. He and I had a great conversation, and we came to an agreement. Nothing had to change with my friends and me, but if anything important happened, he would be my first text or call.

This simple communication plan increased the intimacy in our marriage so effectively that we've been practicing it for years. It has even worked as a connection builder in my prayer life. If anything happens that registers high on my emotional scale or seems important, I pray first. God is my first "call," then Mike, and then anyone else. This simple order of communication has reinforced my priorities of connection and helps me remember to pray in the moment before I react.

Finally, I am most present when I pray to God *as a person*.

I recently got an e-mail from a professional connection, and although my name was in the subject line and the e-mail was addressed to me, I quickly realized it was a form letter. Our brains train themselves to recognize generic language or the tone someone has when they are selling us something. I didn't even finish reading the e-mail.

Similarly, when we pray, there is a temptation to fall into form-letter mode. This is especially true if God is more of a Friend-of-a-friend, met once at a networking event, listed in my contacts folder, but not-sure-if-He'd-remember-me kinda guy. In our form-letter mode, we fall back on formal language: "Lord Jesus." We use words that we've heard other people use like "Holy Spirit, come" or

"I just want to lift up to You" and other things we would never say in an ordinary conversation. We structure our prayers by ticking off a checklist of topics. These formalities are not a way to keep God's name holy, and they distance us from talking to God as if we have a relationship with Him.

My e-mails to my husband are almost always fewer than three lines, and they usually have an emoji.

Why? Because I just talked to Mike that morning. Because I'll probably talk to him again within a few hours. Because our son just told me with a straight face that if he ever met a gingerbread man, he would beat him up and eat him, and I am *cracking up*, and I wanted to share that moment with him.

God desires our love as well as our respect. It's not too casual or an insult to God's holiness for us to call Him "Father" and speak to Him like a person we have a relationship with. That's how Jesus taught us to pray. When Jesus taught His disciples to pray, He wasn't prescribing a form-letter format or teaching them the magic words to a cosmic spell. Jesus put forward a prayer that was simple and direct, with a structure that brings our will, our wants, and our needs into our conversation with God:

Your Father knows what you need before you ask him. This, then, is how you should pray:
"Our Father in heaven,
hallowed be your name,
your kingdom come,
your will be done,
   on earth as it is in heaven.
Give us today our daily bread.

And forgive us our debts,

as we also have forgiven our debtors.

And lead us not into temptation,

but deliver us from the evil one." (Matthew 6:8–13)

In the Lord's Prayer, Jesus teaches us to pray, "*Your kingdom come, your will be done.*" It is less important for us to *know* God's will than it is for us to *want* God's will: *Teach us, God, to want what You want.* I used to think God's will was a single path that was easy to lose if you took too many steps off to the side. I saw God's will as a hiking path that was missing its signs at the splits, and if I went the wrong way, I'd fall off a cliff. Even worse, God seemed coy or secretive regarding His will. I had to pray really hard to figure anything out, and even then He didn't always answer me. My life seemed to hang in the balance every time I considered college, named my major, or went on a date. I wanted God to help me make good decisions.

And I'm not alone. Scripture tells of people casting lots, asking for signs, and wanting to know God's specific word for a specific decision. Sometimes He is very clear in His plan (2 Samuel 5:23–24), and sometimes He is not. Actually, when the Bible talks about God's will, it usually refers to His plan of salvation (1 Timothy 2:4; 2 Peter 3:9) or the kinds of lives we live (Micah 6:8; Ephesians 5:15–20; 1 Thessalonians 4:3; 5:18). God's will is more often about who we are than what we do. When we see the concept of God's "calling" in the New Testament, we are called to be disciples (Matthew 4:20–22), called to salvation (2 Thessalonians 2:14), called to be sons and daughters (1 John 3:1; Ephesians 1:5), and called to be a people of God (1 Corinthians 1:2). God calls us to relationship before He calls us to action. Beth Moore puts it this way: "Seek the caller, not the calling, and you will run smack into your calling."

Life with God is supposed to be anxious for nothing (Philippians 4:6), so we'd be crazy to think that He intends for us to be anxious about every decision we make, especially the ones we don't hear a clear response to right away. God's will provides a lot of free space for us to exercise our own judgment and take into account our own desire. Sometimes when I'm with my kids at the grocery store, I'll let them pick what's for dinner and teach them how to wind through the aisles and shop for those ingredients. I'm just as happy when my kids want tacos as when they want spaghetti, but cupcakes don't fly. I'm more than happy to let them choose within certain boundaries. So, unless God has made it clear that you should make a certain decision, don't worry. This time is a chance to talk to God, search for wisdom, and make your own decision. You want to know God's will, but He also wants you to learn how to walk in the freedom He has given you.

> God's will is more often about who we are than what we do.... God calls us to relationship before He calls us to action.

It's not always easy to pray for God's will to be done.

When my sister-in-law Julia had her fourth baby, we were ecstatic! My three wild nephews would finally have a little sister to look after. Only weeks after my niece was born, though, Julia was diagnosed with brain cancer. When my brother told me the news, his face was determined but afraid.

I couldn't imagine Julia gone. I couldn't imagine what that

would do to my young nephews, to my brother. I couldn't imagine my newborn niece not knowing her amazing mama. I tried—I tried so hard—to pray, "Thy will be done." I gained a new appreciation for the agony of Jesus's prayer the night before He died. I didn't necessarily want God's will to be done. I wanted Julia to be healed. I didn't know how to pray. I wanted the cancer to be gone, but praying for a giant tumor to disappear was scary. What if God didn't heal Julia? Praying for God's will felt a little safer; whatever happened would be an answer then. I could protect my hope and insulate my faith from disappointment.

And I had been disappointed before.

My dad was diagnosed with the exact same brain cancer Julia had. He had been dead for nearly a decade when her tumor glowed white on the scan. I'm not sure what gave me courage to pray for her healing. Maybe I trust God more now, or maybe I could too easily see myself in her place.

I hadn't even prayed for my dad to be healed.

He was terminal, and all signs pointed to death. The doctor didn't even have to say, "Six months."

My husband (boyfriend back then) was driving that night. We were on my way to my parents' house when my mom called. I remember the exact curve in the freeway with its tall poles that had orange lights on top; I remember the exact place where the world went wiggly. My old cell phone that still had buttons on it was pushed against my cheek. Mom was trying to sound matter-of-fact and positive at the same time. But when she said, "Cancer," my body knew the truth before I even had time to think: my dad was going to die. I couldn't tell if the orange lights were moving in slow motion or fast, and my head almost hit the dashboard as it fell between my knees. I couldn't cry. I couldn't breathe. I threw up in my car.

During the weeks that followed, I only prayed for two things. Both a little selfish, I guess, looking back.

1. God, please let Dad live until my wedding day.
2. God, please let Dad's brain work clearly for just a minute. Let us be able to say goodbye.

My dad and I had been dreaming of my wedding day since I was little. I used to think it was normal for dads to want to practice walking down the aisle and dancing a first dance with their nine-year-old daughters, but I'm not so sure it's a widespread practice. Mike and I moved our wedding date up. We knew Dad would probably be in a wheelchair, but it felt like our last chance to celebrate with him. He had between six and nine months to live, so we planned our wedding for four months out.

Dad's tumor blocked meaning from his words. The look in his eyes made it seem like he was trying to say something, but the random selection of slurred words coming from his mouth was impossible to translate. He'd say things like, "Shout forth" or "piggyyyy . . . lucky warm" and then wait in annoyed expectation as if we were all idiots who were refusing to help him. "Umm, did you mean you want a blanket?" His raised eyebrows would furrow, and he would be angry.

God, my relationship with my dad is so complicated. Please, just give us like sixty seconds, maybe two minutes. You don't have to save his life, but please just push back the fog. Let us say goodbye. Let us say, "I'm sorry" and "I forgive you." Let us say, "I love you."

I kept waiting for my moment, the kind that Nicholas Sparks describes near the end of *The Notebook*. It never came. Dad died ten weeks before my wedding day.

WAS IT SO MUCH TO ASK?!?! TOO MUCH?!?! Would it have changed the course of history so drastically? God, I let You take my dad! I didn't even complain! It's not like I'm asking for a convertible. How could You deny me such simple requests?

I had pushed hope far away; I had never even asked for healing. I was happy to settle for scraps, and even those were denied me. The polite brownnose prayers were over. I shook my fist at heaven and didn't listen for God's response. I needed to work on steeling my resolve, on thickening my skin. This hurt too much. Hope, I decided, was a placebo. I was determined never to touch it again. I was deeply disappointed. God had been dangerously ineffective (I didn't want to be forced to admit this), and life is unfair (it's hard to keep living with this in the front of your mind). Nope. Not worth it. Hope should come with a warning label that reads, "Hedge your bets, dummy." And it does come with a warning label, but that label reads, "Beware of counterfeits."

> We can rejoice, too, when we run into problems and trials, for we know that they help us develop endurance. And endurance develops strength of character, and character strengthens our confident hope of salvation. And this hope will not lead to disappointment. For we know how dearly God loves us, because he has given us the Holy Spirit to fill our hearts with his love. (Romans 5:3–5 NLT)

There is a hope that doesn't ever disappoint, but there's only one—the hope that God will save us, and that He is saving us. That He will make all things right one day, and that He is making things right even now. Hope is like a muscle, and it has to be made stronger. When we experience pain, that can build our endurance. When we learn to keep pushing through even when we want to quit, it builds our character. It takes a strong character to practice hope in a dark world and not give in to helplessness or cynicism. But hope is not a sham, as long as our hope is in God. We will never be disappointed by the saving grace He offers, because He loves us. If we want to be hopeful people, we have to be ready for our hope muscle to be made stronger. That's why Paul tells us to celebrate problems and unanswered prayers; they are building our resiliency and developing our deep hopefulness. In the end, we won't be disappointed.

I learned later that there was a lot I didn't know about my dad and the time surrounding his death, information that explained why everything felt so strange. I still don't know why God didn't give me the two things I prayed for, but I do know that unanswered prayer is not proof that hope is a sham. It's not proof that God is blind or uncaring. I don't have to protect God's reputation, and I don't have to wall up my heart.

Paradoxically, in my hope unmet, I met hope I didn't have to be afraid of. God is good, He loves me, and even if He doesn't always save me from pain, He makes it count. Sometimes the best gift He can give me is not to immediately make me happy, but to ultimately make me stronger.

My friend Bronwyn Lea taught me a better way to pray, more in line with the surest hope we have: "Instead of praying, 'God, make it better,' I need to pray, 'God, make it count.'"

God, Your will is bigger than Julia being healed or not being healed. You have desires and plans for what this sickness is going to do in her life, in each of our lives. God, please spare her life. God, please heal her brain. God, please let her raise her children and let her children be loved by their mother. Don't let us be glad only after we are through this sickness and she is healed. Do something even now. Make it count.

It was a terrifying journey, one my brother would call the biggest test of faith in his life. After many tears and much darkness, Julia and my brother came out the other side saying, "It is well with my soul." The cancer had counted. They had an unprecedented experience of the nearness of God, the love of the people around them, and the limits of their faith being met with limitless grace. Julia went into remission, and she is still cancer-free today. She's a glowing wife and mom who challenges me with her gratitude for each day. She knows God's goodness can reach anywhere, and she lives her life unafraid of the dark.

In Jesus's prayer, after He prays, *"Your will be done,"* He teaches us to pray, *"Give us today our daily bread."*

I am a planner, so of course I have a mom purse. If I don't have enough granola bars for everyone in the car plus an extra, I'm slipping. I also like to know that I have enough toilet paper for the year, not just for today. As limitless as God's goodness is, we're supposed to depend on who He is, not on what He has. One way we learn the dependability of God is by trusting Him to give us exactly what we need for today.

This is how God provided food for Israel (Exodus 16:4) and how Jesus says we should deal with our problems (Matthew 6:34): one day at a time. When we live day by day, trusting God to provide what we need, we learn how dependable He is. Every morning we wake up, we can remember that God sustained us the day before and will sustain us again in the new day ahead.

My first experience with depression after pregnancy was scary. After getting much-needed help, I had finally been able to breathe for a while. I was looking at the sky more, and I surprised myself by feeling happy for the smallest reasons. Then December came. It bothered me that I didn't know why the grief came back. That I had to admit that I needed help again. That I couldn't just be healed.

> When we live day by day, trusting God to provide what we need, we learn how dependable He is. Every morning we wake up, we can remember that God sustained us the day before and will sustain us again.

During that tough month, I began to practice the Ignatian prayer of Daily Examen. At the end of each day, I reviewed what happened that day, starting from the most recent memory and moving back toward the morning, praying for God's help to remember and notice. Then I thanked God for the ways He provided for me that day, for the grace I saw in unexpected people and places. Then I prayed specifically for the feelings—good and bad—that stood out. I confessed anything I didn't do but should have or things I did but should not have. I let myself be forgiven. I prayed for the day I would wake up to and for whatever I was worried about. I prayed that I would notice good things and have enough of what I needed to make it through another day. I tried to live one day at a time.

One day at a time, one prayer at a time, I learned to notice that even on days I didn't feel like I had enough or was enough,

God always gave me what I needed. I learned to trust Him and thank Him. Slowly the fear went away, and the gratitude came and stayed.

Jesus teaches us to pray by saying, *"Forgive us our sins, as we have forgiven those who sin against us"* (Matthew 6:12 NLT). I used to hold off on confessing some sins. I felt it disingenuous to confess something when I knew I was probably going to do it again. Also, confession is embarrassing, and saying, "I was wrong" grates against my pride in ways I'd rather avoid. When we offer a heartfelt, true apology—not the kind with caveats and excuses—we are vulnerable. We expose ourselves as imperfect (or actually awful) and ask to be accepted even then; we ask to receive mercy and forgiveness. We yield our authority to the person we've offended and have no control over the response. The person could laugh at us or label us or stop loving us. So why would we ever risk it? Because it's worth it.

Blessed is the one whose transgression is forgiven,
whose sin is covered. . . .
For when I kept silent, my bones wasted away.
(Psalm 32:1, 3 ESV)

Psalm 32 is a beautiful song of the forgiven. We forget how much it weighs on us to carry our sin and guilt around. I've felt the sting of not having someone accept my apology or, worse, having someone forgive me but never letting me forget. God's not like that. He promises to always forgive us. And when He accepts us again and again at our very worst, we start to believe that He truly does love us. Shame can't wrap itself around us if we are constantly

peeling it from our shoulders in confession. When we acknowledge how much we need forgiveness, our hearts soften and become
quicker to forgive others.

God isn't keeping a running tally of every sin, and I'm sure I
haven't confessed every single sin I've committed. Although being forgiven is about making things right with God, it's also about
developing our relationship with Him. When we say, "I'm sorry"
in any relationship, we're saying, "I love you." We're saying that we
want to stay, to work things out. We're saying we want to have a
healthy relationship, not sweep things under the rug. We're saying
that we want to be honest with each other. We're saying that the
other person matters to us more than our saving face or guarding
our pride. When we apologize, we're loving the other person more
than we are loving ourselves. When they forgive us, they are doing
all these same things. And God's forgiveness is one of the many
ways He says, "I love you. Yes, the real you." He teaches us to do the
same so we can all learn mercy.

In Jesus's prayer, He also teaches us to pray, *"Deliver us from
the evil one."*

We might not be slaves to our own broken records anymore,
but sometimes we forget that. We need God to teach us to live in
our freedom and to resist temptation daily. Confessing our sins is
good, but watching for sin and staying away from it will save a lot
of heartache. Temptation is a part of life and can test our faith in
ways that are healthy for us, but God never tempts us (James 1:13).
When we are tempted by the tempter or by our own desires, He
always provides a way out (1 Corinthians 10:13).

In Jesus's prayer lesson, He began by saying, *"Your Father
knows what you need before you ask him."*

Before you begin praying, God has seen you and knows what you need, and these truths can prompt some big questions. Tonight, for instance, my son leaned over and whispered in my ear, "Mama, why doesn't God give us what we want when we pray?"

My heart ached in instant memory of all the times I have asked that same question. If God knows what I need, it seems so cruel that He doesn't give it to me. Yet I can't pray to God and stay angry or accusing for too long because His gentle compassion is too real. Sometimes I can even hear Him whisper, "My heart is broken too."

God's faithfulness is not defined by my fears or failures. His answers to prayer, whatever they may be, are all credits to His goodness, not to His cruelty. As A. W. Tozer reminds us in *The Knowledge of the Holy*, "All God's acts are done in perfect wisdom, first for His own glory, and then for the highest good of the greatest number for the longest time. And all His acts are as pure as they are wise, and as good as they are wise and pure. Not only could His acts not be better done: a better way to do them could not be imagined."

"I don't always know, baby," I tell my son whose shoulders are still slumped in disappointment. "But I know God knows what we need, and He only gives us good things."

That didn't reassure him. He really wanted the Pokémon cards he had prayed for.

HEARING GOD'S VOICE
IN PRAYER

Read through these invitations to hear God speak through prayer. Which practice might help you listen for God's voice?

1. Plug any screens you charge overnight in an outlet away from your bed (you'll still hear the alarm). Instead, place your Bible or a note with a reminder to pray close to where you sleep so your first thought and last thought of the day can be a prayer instead of being swept up by a device.

2. Choose some friends to pray with in person or over the phone this coming week.

3. Be conscious of your body position as you pray. Is there an opportunity for your posture to affect your prayer? Try praying on your face, knees, seated, or standing.

4. What unanswered prayer, if any, have you all but given up on? Or what never-prayed prayer have you been holding back from God? What would happen if you prayed your honest desires, fears, or doubts? Would you try?

CHAPTER 6

A VOICE THAT SPEAKS IN COMMUNITY

We had just moved to a new city, and I had a new baby and no friends. I discovered during this time that it's tough to make new friends when:

1. You don't have a lot of free time because you are keeping a baby human alive.
2. You have spit-up on your shirt and haven't taken a shower in maybe three days.

That's when MOPS (Mothers of Preschoolers) saved my life. I met another mom on the floor of the public library after story hour, and she invited me to come to a MOPS meeting with her. After she said something about free childcare and breakfast, I stopped listening and gave her my phone number.

The very next week I was sitting around a table with incredible women who had all been complete strangers to me before I showed up. I learned people's stories, I learned about sleep training, and

I learned where the zoo was. I was actually making friends, and all of us in our little community needed each other during this crazy time.

Only a couple of months after I joined, I had some sort of allergic reaction to something. My face got all swollen and blotchy, and I was itchy and uncomfortable. I wasn't in anaphylactic shock or anything, but I had blotchy hives all over my body, and my eyes were almost swollen shut. I did not look good, and that's coming from someone whose bar for personal appearance before leaving home was already dangerously low. I called my library/MOPS friend, Nat, and told her I couldn't make it to our table that day.

"I'm just frustrated," I admitted. "I'm trying to figure out how to take care of my baby when I need to take care of myself."

"You know what? I'm going to set up meals for you," Nat said.

I was immediately hesitant. I mean, I'd had a bad allergic reaction, but it's not like I couldn't microwave a couple hot dogs.

"That's nice, but I don't want people to have to do that," I said. "It's hard enough for all of us to make dinner for our own families."

"Liz, this is something we do for each other. When we help each other, it bonds us together. You need to be a little vulnerable and ask for help. People want to help you."

"Okay, but nothing crazy," I relented. "Maybe just today and tomorrow?"

Nat agreed and said she would call the mom who sets up food for everyone. I was actually relieved when I got the e-mail with the meal sign-ups later that day. It was nice to have help.

Until I opened the e-mail.

First off, I had been set up for two weeks of meals, not two days.

Then I read the description, which simply said: "Liz has been in the hospital for a severe rash."

I was so embarrassed. Before, I had felt guilty for getting meals due to a situation that wasn't *really* that dire. Now I felt guilty for getting meals for a situation that wasn't even medically accurate.

Later that day, a mom I had never met before knocked on my door. I didn't know what to do. I thanked her profusely for bringing dinner to us, explaining that it had been such a hard day. She looked at me sympathetically with a tilted head. "Oh, of course. And just so you know, we prayed for you as a group today. I'm so sorry you have a personal rash that makes it hard for you to get around."

My already-red face must have added a few more shades of pink.

My *personal* rash.

I wondered how that played out during the large-group prayer time. . . . "Dear Lord, we just lift up poor Liz and her personal rash. . . ."

It's one thing for a group of people to pray for you. It's another for a group of people—many whose names you don't even know—to pray for God to deliver you from a deeply personal medical condition that you don't even have. And one that absolutely did not require hospitalization.

And yet here was this other woman, with two kids waiting in her car, bringing me dinner. Pretty amazing. Especially considering she really had no way of knowing if my "personal rash" was contagious.

I want Christian community to be where I meet my new best friends, but what I almost always find is much more like the family

God calls us to be. The big, crazy, embarrassing, plenty-of-drama family that loves and needs each other. Some of my best friends and some of my best memories involve people I might have never met if we didn't both know Jesus. Even the church I grew up in, although there was a lot of hurt there, was full of people who loved me well and whom I still love today.

It's more comfortable to talk about community theoretically or even theologically, but it's impossible to talk about community honestly as anything other than deeply personal. Our most intimate communities as well as our unmet desires for belonging have shaped all of us. Community has always been bittersweet for me because it is so dynamic: friendships and friend groups are always changing. Since it takes me a long time to welcome someone into my truest thoughts and feelings, it is a loss worth grieving when a friend distances herself emotionally or moves away.

> I want Christian community to be where I meet my new best friends, but what I almost always find is much more like the family God calls us to be. The big, crazy, embarrassing, plenty-of-drama family that loves and needs each other.

There are two main types of community we experience, community as spiritual friendship and community as a church.

First, spiritual friendship may be the greatest gift we can give, and in giving, it also becomes one of the greatest gifts we receive for ourselves. In his book *Sacred Companions*, David Benner describes the relationship between spiritual friends: "Friends who enjoy soul intimacy never settle for gossip or simple exchange of information. Instead they use the

data of events as springboards for the sharing of feelings, percep-
tions, values, ideas, and opinions. . . . They pay attention to inner
experience, not simply the external world."

When we are lucky enough to have a friend who can walk in
our internal world alongside us, who can freely think out loud with
us, she is in a unique position to speak into our lives for better or
worse. Some of our friends—or sometimes even strangers—speak
God's words directly to us as a prophetic voice, but some voices
carry so much influence in our lives that we give their opinion prophetic weight even when they are not carrying the voice of God.

Almost daily I reach out to my soul friends. Sometimes I am
sharing a truth I understood in a new way or looked at from a fascinating angle, but many more times I am bored or frustrated or
anxious. My friends speak God's words from Scripture to me, and
I hear His voice in theirs when they say things like:

"You are not abandoned."

"There are long stretches of obedient waiting in everyone's
journey with God."

"We see what God is doing right now! You are too close to see
it, but you are growing and things are happening."

We all have to take turns carrying God's voice to one another,
because even though we know the truth, we all forget it. One of the
greatest gifts we can give our friends is listening for God's voice
and noticing His presence—in our lives and in theirs.

We all have the power to speak life to one another, and that's
one reason why God wants us to be part of the church He created.
After all, His church is not an institution. It is a network of relationships and experiences, and everyone has been given a unique
gift by the Holy Spirit to make the whole even better. We come

together to remember and celebrate the goodness of God, to share with others the words and comfort He has given each of us, and to build each other up.

Each of us is a temple for the Holy Spirit, an individual meeting place between God and humans (1 Corinthians 6:19). When we come together, we are not just a gathering of individual bodies or temples. Paul taught that the church all together is like one interdependent body, whose functioning depends on each of the individual parts (Romans 12:4–8; 1 Corinthians 12:12–31). The together-body is more than just a metaphor. When Paul used the plural *you* in 1 Corinthians 3:16 (different from the singular *you* in 6:19), he was saying that our together-body is also a temple for the Holy Spirit: "Don't you know that you yourselves [all together] are God's temple?" God meets with each of us, but He also meets with all of us. Something sacred and holy happens when we are gathered together and the Holy Spirit—in us and among us—works.

Together, we remember and celebrate the goodness of God. Every time we take the bread and the cup together in Communion, we hear God say, "Do this in remembrance of Me," and we remind one another of who Jesus is and what the cross means to us. Every time we see someone get baptized, we hear God say, "You have passed through the waters, and now you share in the resurrection life." We pray together and share God's words with each other through teaching that centers us in the story of God and through worship that calls us to be present in our meeting with God.

The church gathers in small groups as well as large groups. In small groups we can tell one another the stories of God in a unique way. One night, for instance, we four couples—who have shared our lives and our secrets for years at weekly meals in one another's homes—sat around a fire. Dinner was over, and tonight's discussion started with a serious question: "As you've gotten older, what role has doubt played in your faith?"

The question floated in the air, hovering over the fire-pit flames. It was very dark outside, and only an orange glow illuminated our faces. As some of us reclined back and others leaned in, the stories tiptoed out like the pitter of a few raindrops on blacktop. Soon we all sat in each other's rainstorm together. Doubts about the Bible and politics and social issues howled through us and around us like a biting wind.

When the storm finally lost its surge, someone quietly asked, "What experiences have you had with God, or how have you seen Him in the world around you, so that you know for sure He is real and has been involved in your life?"

The stormy wind was completely still. The goodness, gentleness, nearness of God came back to us with the warmth of a fire. We remembered. We shared our stories of God's hand moving over us. As we shared our noticing, we recognized God even more clearly in ourselves and in one another. That situation that worked out, that heart that was changed, that realization that we couldn't have made on our own—we piled our stones of remembrance around the ring of the fire.

Our friends—our Jesus family—help us keep a record of God's voice and active presence in our lives and in their own stories. They remind us of our back-then, they cast a vision for our up-ahead, and they pray when we feel stuck in the darkness of our right-now. God told Israel, "Never forget what I've said and who I am. Pass this truth down." We need our oral tradition, our bonfire stories, and each other not only to hear God now but to remember all He has already said and done for us.

Together, we share the words and comfort God has for each of us. God can use a member of our community to utter just the right words to us at just the right time, but sometimes life stories speak louder than advice. If we can learn to listen to people's stories, to fully embrace their pain as well as their celebration, we may see God's faithfulness come to life in their story.

God doesn't just speak to us through the people in our small community; He also speaks through our church community as a whole. A community can experience the birth of an infant and the death of a friend, a long-awaited promotion and a tragic layoff, all in the same week. And when one part of the body is sick, the whole body suffers and participates in the healing. When one part of the body is strong, the whole body celebrates and thanks God. We all have the responsibility of joining in the pain and celebration of one another. We are a support system that we know we ourselves can fall into one day, and we remind one another that life with God is full of blessings and suffering, faith and doubt. It is less terrifying to hold these truths together when we remind one another that God is in the darkness as much as He is in the dawn.

Over time, we hold more than just one another's joys and pain: we learn to hold one another's confessions as well. In *Life Together*, Dietrich Bonhoeffer explores the guilt of sin that private, silent confession can leave behind: "Who can give us the certainty that, in the confession and the forgiveness of our sins, we are not dealing with ourselves but with the living God? God gives us this certainty through our brother."

There are sins that haunt us, sins that we confess too many

times to count, that we cannot break free of no matter how determined we are. Paul had his "thorn in the flesh" (2 Corinthians 12:7), and we all have our own familiar temptations as well. When our confession is only private, only between us and God, our sin stays in the dark, and so can God's forgiveness. We will always be tempted to doubt whether we are really forgiven for that same sin *again* or if we have any hope of escaping our addictions. This is where our community comes in: we embody to one another the grace and abundant forgiveness of God.

We must, however, be wise about whom we confess to and what we confess. Try to find a trusted leader or mentor who regularly confesses her sins to a mentor. Remember the story of the prodigal son (Luke 15:11–31). The father—representing God—delighted in the repentance of his younger son, but the older son resented the father's grace and harbored judgment. We need fewer self-righteous older brothers to condemn us for our mistakes and more sisters who will wrap their arms around us and affirm our Father's declaration that our sins have been forgiven. When we do not feel forgiven, we need sisters who will cry with us at the feet of Jesus. When we sometimes bear the weight of sin's consequences even after we know we are forgiven, we need our sisters to remind us that God's story for us is good and that He can bring beauty from our ashes.

> There are sins that haunt us, sins that we confess too many times to count. . . . This is where our community comes in: we embody to one another the grace and abundant forgiveness of God.

"Liz," my mentor said as she leaned forward, "if we confess our sins, God is faithful. He will forgive us our sins and cleanse us from all unrighteousness. That's First John 1:9. God is faithful. *Jesus* is faithful. He has forgiven you. Your sin is washed away. Go in peace."

I know God forgives me, but I forget that when I have collapsed under the weight of horrifying accusations that are completely true. I need my sisters to remind me. To point me to the cross when my head is too heavy to look up. Only God can forgive us, but sometimes He says, "I forgive you" most clearly through the voice of our community. Our reconciliation is confirmed by His people's embrace, and we all move forward covered in the grace God has poured down.

Together, we build each other up. Community is not an option for a Jesus follower. Living life with fellow believers is the only way we can become who God is making us to be. As our church's lead pastor, Steve Clifford, says, "It's not difficult to live the Christian life alone. It's impossible."

But God has called us into His family not only for how we can learn from and love each other, but also for how we can annoy and upset each other. God can both reveal and very clearly speak to our pride and selfishness through one another. We might keep our blind spots forever if God weren't kind enough to make all of us ragtag spiritual orphans into brothers and sisters. *Brother* and *sister* imply a special family bond, a time-earned closeness and respect, but if you actually have a brother or sister, you know that a sibling can seriously get under your skin.

I felt this once when I was in a women's small group that I had been dying to join. Our leader was genuinely kind, and the people who came were polite, and there were always snacks. It took me awhile to figure out why I never wanted to go again, why this one woman there irritated me even though she was so sweet.

We just don't click, I thought. *Maybe this group is a little shallow for my mature faith.* (I didn't know back then that mature faith does not condescend, according to Romans 12:3.)

I thought my failure to connect with the group was just a personality clash, until I brought it up to a mentor of mine. He introduced me to the idea of internal furniture.

We all have a sort of arrangement of furniture in our minds. We've arranged it so it feels like our own comfortable home. We have reasons for the size, shape, and order of things, reasons that are all very personal. When we interact with people, it can be like letting them into our living room. Sometimes it's nice to visit with them there, but some people come in and kick their feet up where we don't want them to, or leave their muddy boots on, or actually pick up a chair and move it to the other side of the room and say, "That's better." As the host, we have to choose how we respond.

I had never thought of it that way, but the metaphor was really helpful. Someone messing with my ideas and assumptions gave me the same feeling as someone messing with my stuff. How rude.

"That's it! This one girl has really different values on a certain topic that is personal to me. I feel like she criticized the painting that hung over my imaginary fireplace."

"Well, Liz," he said, looking at me gently, "how are you going to respond?"

"I want to thank her for swinging by, politely escort her to the door, and never invite her over again."

"Okay," he said with understanding. "Now let's remember that Jesus shares your living room and is sitting on the couch as this plays out. How do you think He would respond? And does that change your answer?"

What? Jesus. Right. I almost forgot about Him. He would probably invite her to come sit on the couch, talk about how she understands the world, and then encourage me to share my ideas. Then, if that conversation is anything like His interaction with the woman at the well, He'd ask good questions and be honest and winsome as He explained how He sees things (a viewpoint that would be different from ours and totally true).

> A powerful shift happens when I pray for someone. I start to see that person in relationship to God instead of in relationship to me. Instead of seeing how he annoys me or how she makes me jealous, I see how God loves them.

It is too hard to be like Jesus! Why won't He leave me alone, let me dig in my stubborn heels and only talk to people who agree with me? Why won't He let me be offended when someone agrees with people whom I don't like? Why won't He let me live in my living room alone *with everything arranged just as I want it to be?*

Why? Because He loves me. Because I'm part of His family. Because I have too many things to learn about conflict and forgiveness and grace. Our family, our brothers and sisters, our community—we all drive each other crazy because even though we're God's children, we're still stubborn and selfish and insecure.

God gently speaks to us about our character when we are annoyed, offended, hurt, or angry with each other. Every time someone kicks our furniture, we have an invitation to make our lives a home for Christ instead of a museum for ourselves.

One of the easiest ways we can learn to love even our most difficult siblings is through prayer. We can pray for God to show us what our initial response to them reveals about us, and we can also pray for them. A powerful shift happens when I pray for someone. I start to see that person in relationship to God instead of in relationship to me. Instead of seeing how he annoys me or how she makes me jealous, I see how God loves them, and I sometimes glimpse the work He is slowly and intentionally doing in their lives. I recognize how that is the same holy work that God is doing in my life. Sometimes I can even hear more clearly God's words for a particular situation in my life as I intercede for someone else than when I simply seek the wisdom for myself. When I am praying for someone, I can get out of the way and watch what God is doing. Prayer makes it much easier for me to love people, to celebrate with them, or to cry with them even when I struggle with not being able to help more.

Not only do we have the chance to pray for one another, but we also have the chance to invest in each other. Discipleship is the model Jesus gave us for living the Christian life, and we see it played out in the early church (Titus 2:3–5; 1 Timothy 5:1). It's a good idea to think about who in your community would make a trustworthy mentor as well as who might need you as a mentor. I have a weakness for idolizing mentors: I can find myself going to them for wisdom before I pray about something because I trust them so much. I'm so thankful for my friends who journey with me and say, "Let's pray about that" or "I don't know." The best mentors remind me to be still and notice God's voice in every area of my life. And when I mentor, I am reminded that the wisdom I have to share with others is far short of the goodness of God's wisdom. God speaks through people, but we most clearly hear His voice when our community points us back toward Him.

Always pointing each other to God instead of to ourselves helps us develop healthy attachments. We will not hear what God has to say to us in the context of our community if we are overly attached or under attached to one another. We have to guard ourselves against becoming overly attached to others, and we have to resist the attention of people who want to become overly attached to us. Being overly attached to someone undermines healthy growth and personal independence. On the other hand, being under attached doesn't allow the intimacy necessary for healthy discussions or growth-promoting conflict. If we are too distant from commitment or church, or if we only rely on virtual connections, the depth and breadth of our faith are at risk. But if we are too dependent on a person or a church, we won't fully develop the depth of our relationship with God.

As Francis Chan notes, "We've become experts at gathering Christians around great bands, speakers, and events. Where we have failed is in teaching believers how to be alone with God" (DesiringGod.org). If we are going to be people who help each other hear God's voice, we have to learn when to get out of the way. A baby otter helped me understand this.

I often took our kids to explore the magic at the Monterey Bay Aquarium when they were young. (I think I loved it more than they did.) On one trip, we learned about little Luna, an abandoned sea otter pup that was rescued by the aquarium staff. The goal of any rescue there is to prepare the animal to be released back into the wild. As they told Luna's story, they showed a picture of her eating from a bottle. The feeder was wearing a black welding mask, black cape, and big black gloves. It was strange to watch a giant black blob monster feeding the cutest, cuddliest, sweetest otter baby in the world. It almost looked cruel.

Anticipating the question that was arising in each of us, the docent told us that the reason they feed the otters this way is so that they don't bond with the keepers or think of them as their mothers. Otherwise the baby otter won't be prepared to leave and go back into the wild. This illustrates one of the hardest things about Christian community: being known and vulnerable but knowing when to keep the welder mask on. Even as we serve one another, love one another, and bless one another, our dependence on each other should not be growing as much as our dependence on God does. After all, we human beings will only let each other down. The goal of us worshipping together, helping one another, and belonging to each other is so that each of us can become more dependent on God.

When I'm watching out for overdependence or under-dependence, there are two red flags I pay attention to:

1. The feeling that I could wash my hands and completely walk away on a minute's notice.
2. The feeling that I am desperately clinging to a person or group of people and would collapse without their friend-ship, love, and support.

Depending on the day, I am equally vulnerable to both unhealthy attachments. Do you have one you more easily fall into? Whichever weakness you may have, learn to notice it happening. Let God speak to you about it and to heal the wounds. Develop your attachment to God. What would a healthy independence look like for your stage of faith? Ask your community to help you move in that direction.

As much as we want to love each other, we will always fail one another. Just as there is no such thing as a perfect person, there is definitely no such thing as a perfect Christian community—everyone's imperfections are in the mix.

That's one reason why you don't have to look far to find conflict or hurt in most Christian communities. Even in the apostle Paul's letters to the very first churches, we see racism, feuding, elitism, taking sides, and people who call themselves believers acting nothing at all like Jesus. It's a disappointing thread throughout church history that is still evident today. It's hard to imagine how God can allow emotional abuse, sexual abuse, financial corruption, or prejudice to exist in His church, whom He loves. Unfortunately, when the people of God are the face of God, they can make Him look very ugly.

In John 2:13–17, Jesus turned over tables at the temple, but before He did that, He "made a whip out of cords, and drove all from the temple courts" (v. 15). The image of Jesus brandishing a whip and terrifying everyone in sight was not easy for me. Until I realized whom Jesus was railing against. You see, I know what it's like to feel unprotected by God in His own house. It is outrageous to me the level of imperfection that God is comfortable with, both in His church and in me.

Since the leadership of the church I grew up in presented themselves as divinely appointed shepherds and none of them were struck down by lightning, I assumed that God was okay with everything that was going on. After college, I walked away from the experience confused and secretly angry, but I also was deeply afraid to explore my anger, because I thought I was angry at God. But Jesus with a whip frees me from being angry at God and gives me permission to explore and express my anger toward systems and even people who stand in the way of people (like me) coming to Him. Those tables Jesus turned over had been set up at the temple for some time. That was definitely not the first day of exploitation or exclusion in those temple courts. It's unclear why God allowed the predatory economics to happen at the temple up until then, but Jesus made it crystal clear how He felt about it.

Unhealthy church communities cause deep hurt, and some of us are still waiting for Christ to come to the rescue. Even in relatively healthy churches we can sabotage our own experience with our expectations of what church can do for us. Our time together—our time as a community—should be fueled by our time alone with God, and our time alone with God should be enriched by our time in community. In fact, our relationship with Jesus is actually the heart of Christian community. As individualistic as our personal relationship with Jesus has become, many of us use our time in church or group Bible study as our only time listening for and to God's voice. We depend on group

> Our time together—our time as a community—should be fueled by our time alone with God, and our time alone with God should be enriched by our time in community.

worship to inspire us, and we forget to worship God when the band isn't there. Unless we spend time alone with God, we won't be able to thrive in community. We won't have anything to give, and we'll have crazy expectations of what we should receive spiritually. If we are hungry for strong community connection, first we have to get alone with God. Our time with Him will give us what we need so we can give to others, and it will also keep us grounded so we can confront unhealthy community patterns when they come up.

Healthy community, characterized by mutual trust and vulnerability, isn't just found; it's created over time. We have to extend trust and be genuine with others before we experience the depth of intimacy we hope for. We have to intentionally build relationships and stick to them. Spiritual friendships are one of the kindest gifts of God. We can't come to community to mine for friendships, but when we love everyone around us and share our spiritual triumphs and pain with each other, very deep friendships often form.

We live in Silicon Valley, and we love our city. Like many urban areas, though, we face two key challenges when it comes to community. First is the transient population: people are constantly coming and going from all over the world. Second, whether you are working two jobs to scrape by or you have a gig at the hottest company in the Valley, everyone is insanely busy.

Putting priority on intentional community is one of the strongest lights we shine in what the Barna Research Group has identified as the least churched area in the United States. Exercising generous hospitality and modeling the values of Sabbath rest go completely against the values of our area. Hospitality and rest are also the most grace-filled gifts we can give our isolated and lonely, busy and stressed-out neighbors. God doesn't just use Christian community to speak to us; He's speaking through our communities to the world we live in.

Our Christian community is not just our friends or our church or our denomination. As followers of Jesus, our family is *much* bigger than that. We have brothers and sisters all over the world. We are responsible to hold their joy and their pain with them as well: there is only one body of believers that we are all a part of. God is calling us all to do the work of His kingdom both individually and together. We will hear God's voice when we listen for Him *with* each other, *for* each other, and *through* each other. We hear His words and respond to them together.

HEARING GOD'S VOICE
IN COMMUNITY

Read through these invitations to hear God speak through community. Which practice might help you listen for God's voice?

1. Make an effort to connect in person with the church or Christians near you. What would it look like to take a next step toward deeper connection?

2. What do you think characterizes a healthy mentorship? Spend intentional time with someone who is older than you and also with someone who is younger than you.

3. Do you have an opportunity to celebrate with someone who is celebrating or to grieve with someone who is grieving? If you're hesitant, what's keeping you from contacting that person? What can you do to overcome that barrier?

4. Is there peace that needs to be made in any of your relationships? Look for an opportunity to practice confession or extend forgiveness.

CHAPTER 7

A VOICE THAT SPEAKS IN OUR DAILY LIVES

n her poem "Black Rook in Rainy Weather," Sylvia Plath (1932–63) reflects on everyday miracles and how the radiance of the sunlight might land on something as ordinary as a kitchen table "bestowing largesse, honor, one might say love." As she winds her words to an end, she concludes, "Miracles occur, if you care to call those spasmodic tricks of radiance miracles." Our ordinary lives are full of those "tricks of radiance." God's glory sometimes comes to us in majesty and splendor, shining brightly in our memories as an encounter with something so Other and so Divine that the moment cannot be otherwise explained. Most times, God's glory shines in a sliver of light across the table piled high with cereal bowls. Or it sparkles like a brief glint of brightness in a conversation.

Jesus—God with us—spent many unrecorded days in sawdust and waiting, always aware of His Father in heaven. His Spirit in me means that God is with me in my routines, my emotions, my ambitions, and my living room. I had never thought to listen for His words in my most ordinary places. I had never noticed the rays of light on the kitchen table that Sylvia wrote about because I hadn't been looking for miracles there.

When the kids were young, I was eager to find that light on the table, to name it, to grab on to its promise that I wasn't alone or forgotten, but everything on my kitchen table seemed to point to the complete opposite idea. Not only the dishes from last night's dinner, but the *wrappers* from dinner the night before, cluttered my view, all of it proof of my failure.

One afternoon I was washing dishes, and every plate, bowl, pan, and utensil we owned must have been on the counter because I have never seen such high, wobbly stacks. My stomach sank, and I let out a deep sigh. As I pulled out a plastic container from the pile, I made the mistake of removing the lid, discovering rotting food still inside and almost throwing up in the sink full of soaking pots. Gripping the edge of the counter with two white-knuckled hands, I let out a violent but silent scream in my head. I imagined myself ripping off an apron (that I wasn't actually wearing), stomping up to my invisible boss (that I didn't have), and telling him that I was a strong, capable, intelligent woman, and he could find someone else to wash his dirty dishes.

In that moment, an image flashed: Jesus looking up at me with a towel around His waist. On the floor, scrubbing the assaulting smell of old manure and blood off of His disciples' feet. Serving His family.

You call me "Teacher" and "Lord," and rightly so, for that is what I am. Now that I, your Lord and Teacher, have washed your feet, you also should wash one another's feet. I have set you an example that you should do as I have done for you. Very truly I tell you, no servant is greater than his master, nor is a messenger greater than the one who sent him. Now that you know these things, you will be blessed if you do them. (John 13:13–17)

It was as if my Lord handed me back the apron I had thrown at Him and invited me to join Him right where He was, down on the floor and holding a towel. He was not too worthy to serve the ones God had given Him to care for. I was not a slave in this household; I was an embodiment of the love of Christ.

To be honest, I didn't see it that day, but looking back I see it clearly, an almost imperceptible glow of glory that could shine only from the dirtiest dish. God wanted me to have a dish in my hand when He whispered His invitation to serve. A radical bestowing of honor on my ordinary and daily routine, a deeper understanding of Jesus. My Jesus didn't hang on to importance or comfort or privilege, but He came to serve in hard and humble ways. My martyr's stance at the sight of a stack of dishes was suddenly insane. I pulled the dish towel from the handle on which it hung and fell to my knees to pray. Convicted, humbled, invited, enlightened, loved—it's a strange combination that uniquely marks the voice of God. Convicting, but not condemning. Piercing and grace-filled. Heavy and bright. Sacred and ordinary.

We're more likely to notice God's voice in our ordinary, everyday life if we are already listening to His voice in prayer and Scripture. The more we listen to His clear and direct words, the easier it is to recognize His subtle presence with us. The more we pay attention to our very boring routines and habits, the more clearly God can speak to our heart through Scripture and prayer. Ordinary life and time with God both feed off of, and fuel, each other. Most of us compartmentalize our time with God, whether it is just at church gatherings or even if it is a daily devotional practice. God doesn't want our Sunday mornings or even our every morning. He wants us to live our whole lives with Him, in a constant awareness of His presence and love.

Being loved by God doesn't come easily to me, which might be why I was so stunned by this verse from the minor prophets when I came across it in my reading:

> For the LORD your God is living among you.
> He is a mighty savior.
> He will take delight in you with gladness.
> With his love, he will calm all your fears.
> He will rejoice over you with joyful songs.
> (Zephaniah 3:17 NLT)

This characterization of God is so tender and encouraging that it captured my attention for weeks. I tried to wrap my mind around God delighting in me. Being strong and mighty, but glad and joyful at the same time. I even dared to imagine what His singing voice sounded like. It was a fun thought exercise and a meaningful meditation. There is a song based on that verse, and I found myself singing it as I walked, pushing my double stroller. Still, over and over, it was always an "I wonder. . . ."

It's hard to move beyond broken images and impressions of God. The images of Him in the pamphlets at the church I grew up in depicted a faceless giant on a huge throne. I knew He loved me because Jesus died on the cross, but I didn't necessarily think He'd like me too much up close. My greatest hope was for His mercy and grace. I had never dreamed of basking in His joy and delight. Even after weeks of meditating on Zephaniah, I still couldn't picture it.

Until one ordinary day as I sat on the couch feeding my youngest. Laundry heaps were shoved to the corner beside me, and plastic toys were strewn all over the floor. My sweet daughter had a habit of stealing my attention while I was trying to take care of her little brother, but today she was sitting on the rug, quietly content. She wasn't eighteen months old yet and hadn't started talking. She still felt like my baby even though her new brother made her look enormous in contrast. She picked up a baby doll and cooed softly at the undressed toy. She picked up a little bottle and tenderly put it to the doll's mouth. Then she set the bottle down and held the baby close to her chest. She softly rocked it, and shushed it, and hummed a tune I didn't recognize. Maybe her own song. Her action was the simplest thing in the world, but three feet in front of me my little girl captured all my attention. With that baby in her arms, she looked so nurturing, tender, and kind.

> Most of us compartmentalize our time with God. . . . God doesn't want our Sunday mornings or even our every morning. He wants us to live our whole lives with Him, in a constant awareness of His presence and love.

Although the "mighty savior" imagery in Zephaniah is battle imagery, I needed this cluttered-living-room version to fully see what powerful delight looks like. What is stronger to a baby than his mother? The look of sheer delight as a mama stares into her baby's eyes is one of my favorite things on earth to witness. Her gentle calming of fears. A mother's song over a baby declares her presence, her authority, her loving attention. Just as God uses wet clay and oil and axe heads and all manner of household objects in Old Testament prophecies, He said something powerfully to me through the image of my daughter and her baby doll.

And at that moment, I felt God's eyes on me and heard Him say, "I am just as crazy delighted, protective, and joyful when I hold you, sweet daughter. You are Mine." And looking down at my infant in my arms, I understood that when I hold my babies with strength and joy, I can uniquely show them something about how wonderful God is. Feeding time was over, so I set my son down and swooped up my little girl in my arms, nuzzling my nose into her soft, squishy neck.

"Look! I'm holding a baby who's holding a baby!" and I sang a silly song to her and her dolly, knowing we were all being held in strength, joy, and fearless belonging.

She squealed and wiggled, unamused and unaware of the magic of the moment. We were all right back in our ordinary day. My Scripture meditation helped me notice what God was showing me in my messy living room, and my wild toddler helped me notice what God was showing me in His Word.

My messy living room was an unlikely place for God to speak, but I was far more surprised the first time I heard Him speak over my messy thoughts and emotions. In a sermon once, a pastor asked us to imagine that we were all walking around with screens above our heads that showed a running video of what was going on in our minds. No, thank you! Those thoughts and emotions are for my brain only. Yet there is no place that God cannot speak, especially places so full of raw soul material as thoughts and emotions are.

On one small, boring, and unimportant day, my whole world seemed to be shrinking into invisibility. With one child napping and the other eating in my arms, I retreated to my favorite escape: social media. No one on the other side of my screen could see that I hadn't showered and my pants didn't fit. As I scrolled through the endless stream of pictures, I stopped at one that looked like it had been clipped from *Vogue* magazine. It was my friend Magnolia. She's always been beautiful and elegant and successful; she's got an ambitious drive and a wit that few can challenge. In our twenties, she was one of my best friends, and she always held the bar for success a little higher in a way that motivated me to push myself. I loved that about her.

There she was, elegantly draped like a model against a doorway, looking out at Europe, with her infant sitting on the tile floor beside her. For the first time, I felt my cell phone judging me. It was possible to have a baby and a gorgeous body and leave your house for so much more than the grocery store. I just wasn't doing it right. My insecurity flamed quickly into red-hot jealousy, like a match had been dropped on the gasoline I didn't know was inside me. I tried to scroll past, I tried to get the image out of my mind, I tried not to think of what she had that I didn't, but the more I tried, the more obsessive and bitter I became.

The next night I thought I might find some satisfaction when my friend Avery came over. As she tucked herself into the corner of my couch, the first words out of her mouth were, "Did you see Maggie's picture?"

"Yes. Yes, I did."

"Wasn't it the most beautiful thing you've ever seen?" Avery asked, taking a very different tone than I'd hoped. I was in the mood to commiserate, but she snapped me right out of it as she continued.

"Do you remember how long we prayed for that healthy baby? Seeing that picture felt like proof that God answers prayers. I am trying so hard to believe that there's a picture like that in my future, that I'll have my own prayers-come-true moment."

I was struck by my own darkness. Of course I remembered praying for that baby and for Maggie through months and tears. How could I forget to celebrate that? How could I miss all the beauty of that picture? I prayed that night, "Lord, I am so sorry. I let jealousy take over when I should have been happy for my friend and thankful to You. I don't want to be jealous anymore."

Yet, in the months that followed, no matter how often I prayed, jealousy continued to consume me. It soured friendships, made me glare at myself in the mirror, and ran a torturous spin cycle in my mind of what I wanted and all the things I could never be, do, or have.

I prayed, I made gratitude lists, and I intentionally left kind notes and spoke words of encouragement to my friends who were doing well. But jealousy was a worm inside me that wouldn't die, and it was eating me alive from the inside out. "Lord! Just take this feeling away!"

Jealousy can torture, but it can also teach. Each of our dark emotions is on a thread that connects us to something deeper we may not be aware of: jealousy reveals desire, fear reveals insecurity, anger reveals pain. Like a good Father, God knew that my struggle with jealousy was an opportunity for me to see the things about myself that He already knew. I vaguely remembered praying, "Search my heart, Lord" months earlier in an echo of the psalms.

Well, He had searched and found, and now He was speaking hard, important truth back to me. I saw my own darkness in a way I hadn't recognized before. I saw the way that darkness could consume me, and I saw my desperate need for grace. I saw the way I had clung to a false sense of identity in my success, my appearance, and my adventurous spirit. Now that I was in a season where none of those things was a strength, I was deeply insecure. God was inviting me to a new, truer identity and to greater security in Him. I saw the way my insecurity could affect not only me but those around me. I saw myself poison and sabotage friendships in ways I deeply regret. I felt my powerlessness to be perfect—or even a good person—for the very first time.

But God didn't leave me in a place of disgust with myself and gratitude for His grace. He continued to peel back the layers of my jealousy to reveal insightful truths I would have never discovered had He waved His hand and taken the jealousy away instantly. *What was driving this reaction to Maggie? What did I want so badly?* It was time to consider the desires that drive me and the motives behind those desires. *Why did I want to travel?* Lots of good reasons, but mainly because I felt trapped and thus fantasized about an escape. *Why did I want to post a perfect image of my baby and me?* I thought people thinking I had my life together might take away the sting of absolutely not having everything together.

That's when my prayers changed. No longer confessing sin or making a desperate plea, I went to God holding the things about myself that most scared me. The parts of me that feared rejection the most. He spoke rest into my soul. Deep rest.

Clearly, God can use our emotions to reveal truth to us, truth about who we are and about who He is. I'm not talking about just "feeling God" or having an emotional experience. God uses all of our emotions—good and bad—flowing out of our heart and revealing what is inside. I think of the rebellious prophet Jonah and how angry he was that God forgave his enemies. God gently created a situation that revealed Jonah's compassion for a plant. When the plant died, God showed Jonah through his emotions the grief God Himself would feel if His people perished. Jonah's story is left open-ended. We're not sure if he ever caught on to what God was showing him through his own anger and compassion. Our stories are open-ended too. We have these big feelings of lust and greed and jealousy and depression and fear that feel heavy and inconvenient. In some cases, God Himself may orchestrate situations to bring certain emotions to the forefront of our lives so He can help us deal with them, and so we can hear what He has to say to us about our triggers and fears. Instead of wishing our feelings away, let's take our emotions to God as they arise and ask if He has something to say to us.

Wishing and praying away uncomfortable emotions is only one way I try to ignore what God is saying to me in my daily life. I am also forever searching for a way to make my body cooperate with all I need it to do. I can't count how many times I've asked God to give me strength so I won't be so tired or health so I can finally kick a lingering cold. I'm always trying to be a hero, and I too easily find opportunities to prove myself. I end up staying up too late, stressing out too much, not taking care of myself, and I end up exhausted. I get headaches. I gain weight. My heavy eyelids, my tight shoulders, and my pounding temples try desperately to get my attention, but I am practiced at ignoring them.

My body is a Sabbath meter. I think I need to push forward, achieve, conquer, and never disappoint my family, my friends, or even complete strangers. It's not just that I need to rest so I don't burn out. I need to trust God for my identity and for His provision so I *can* rest. My body is God's messenger that tells me when I am trying too hard and trusting too little.

Getting sick, for instance, reminds me to slow down. A walking boot on my pulled tendon reminds me that every part of my body is affected by the awkward way I walk when it's on. And I am learning it's okay to feel limited and for my world to revolve around my foot because I'm healing.

I know silence, open space, and breathing room are important. I try to get these in small quantities every day, but occasionally my body invites me to make more space—more space for healing, more space for resting, more space for stillness. Having friends who ask me what I'm doing to care for myself and who model caring for their own bodies and souls is helping me a lot. (I still hate it when I face my own limitations.)

My friend Dawn loves to quote Psalm 16:6—"The boundary lines have fallen for me in pleasant places; surely I have a delightful inheritance." The psalmist is saying that God has carved out a space for him, and it's a good one. He doesn't need to push further. We live in a culture that pressures us to be good at everything and constantly busy, but God is offering to help us set good boundaries. I'm still learning to appreciate His reminders in my body.

All of our ordinary days matter to God, and that's good, because ordinary days make up most of our life. When we're only listening for God's fireworks, we'll miss out on the chance to live our life fully with Him the other 99 percent of the time. Our thoughts, our feelings, and our bodies are all opportunities for God to bring things to our attention.

Sometimes God's voice breaks into our lives in ways that feel dramatic, through visions or dreams. Those are very personal experiences, and depending on what sort of Christian culture they worship in, many people hesitate to share their experiences of dreams and visions.

It shouldn't surprise us that God still speaks through dreams and visions. Through the entire story of Scripture, God consistently used dreams and visions to communicate: Joseph, Daniel, Peter, and John are only a few of those whom God spoke to that way. Dreams, visions, and any startling experiences of God's voice are not marks of Christian maturity or signs of the Holy Spirit in a special way. They are simply some of the many ways God breaks into our ordinary and gets our attention.

Did you know, for instance, that in the Middle East God is speaking powerfully through dreams right now? A missionary reported back to our church this summer about two of the underground church pastors he mentors. They are passionately leading their churches at incredible risk to themselves and their families. They come from different parts of the region and different sects of Islam, but both former Muslims have one thing in common: both men heard the good news of Jesus for the first time in a dream. They had known of Jesus from a Muslim perspective, but when He visited them in a dream, they recognized for the first time who He actually is.

Also a missionary, Pastor Tom Doyle served in the Middle East and central Asia full time for eleven years. In his book *Dreams and Visions*, he tells many stories of Muslims encountering Jesus directly in unreachable places. He reports that these dreams are so common that in Egypt an ad was published in the *Cairo Times* newspaper with a hotline for people to call if they had seen in their dreams a man in a white robe.

God is still speaking through dreams today and not only in extreme situations. We can hear His voice in our dreams as well. Maybe a dream offers fresh revelation, or an ordinary dream simply gives our subconscious space to process and explore. It is clear in the Scripture that God has the power to interject Himself into any dream.

Dreams, visions, and any startling experiences of God's voice are not marks of Christian maturity or signs of the Holy Spirit in a special way. They are simply some of the many ways God breaks into our ordinary and gets our attention.

Though the exact meaning of dreams or the weight they should hold in our waking day has been debated, great thinkers across the disciplines of philosophy, psychology, science, and religion have always held them to be significant. The biggest questions have been:

1. Is the source of dreams internal, external, or both?
2. Can dreams be accurately interpreted?

Aristotle and Plato believed dreams were communications from the soul of man, not words or messages from God. In Christian tradition, St. Augustine and Thomas Aquinas believed dreams could come from within or from outside forces, and that not only could God speak to us through dreams but that Satan could influence our dreams as well. Biographies of St. Francis of Assisi describe vivid dreams that he believed were God's direct messages, and he followed their leading. Martin Luther recorded that he experienced dreams of profound spiritual significance throughout the Reformation. John Calvin and John Wesley also wrote and taught about God's voice coming through dreams.

"Do you think dreams actually mean something?" a friend once asked me.

With thousands of years of historic accounts in Scripture, church tradition, and up through the modern day, many would attest that nightly dreams are influenced by not only our internal selves but also the spiritual forces of heaven and hell. A Christian understanding of dreams is that:

1. Dreams can be both internally or externally generated.
2. Interpretations must be prayerfully sought out with discernment.
3. Meanings are not always known the morning after a dream (in the famous Old Testament account of Joseph with his brightly colored coat, the dreams he had took a lifetime to understand).

We see dreams everywhere in the Bible, and many of us have had special dreams of our own—but it is hard to find a credible framework to interpret or understand what is happening when we dream, let alone discern if it is God's voice.

Western Christianity has been so influenced by rationalism

and the intellectual emphasis of the Enlightenment era it's hard to feel serious when discussing divine revelation in dreams. Additionally, the people who seem to speak the loudest about dreams and interpretations love to label themselves as prophets and have a lot of books and services to sell.

> "I have heard what the prophets say who prophesy lies in my name. They say, 'I had a dream! I had a dream!' How long will this continue in the hearts of these lying prophets, who prophesy the delusions of their own minds? . . . Let the prophet who has a dream recount the dream, but let the one who has my word speak it faithfully. For what has straw to do with grain?" declares the LORD. "Is not my word like fire," declares the LORD, "and like a hammer that breaks a rock in pieces?" (Jeremiah 23:25–29)

There have been false prophets declaring their dreams since the days of Jeremiah. That does not mean that all dreams are false. Do you hear the Lord's response? Those false dreams have nothing to do with Him, or the dreams He gives. They are straw and grain, or apples and oranges. His words are fire, and a hammer. They are strong and stand above and aside from ordinary dreams or false dreams.

If God's words are like a powerful hammer and fire, a dream with His words should be clearly recalled and likely remembered for a very long time. The dream may be convicting, but should always leave one hopeful. The meaning should be consistent with God's voice in Scripture and other areas of your life and confirmed in multiple ways.

While the Western world has largely ignored the role of God's voice in dreams, our brothers and sisters in other countries have been studying and researching dreams with far more attention. The Zambian natives devoured their Bibles when missionaries first arrived with the gospel. They read in the Bible so much regarding dreams and visions and fasting that they were left confused when the missionaries dismissed much of it. Nelson Osamu Hayashida, in *Dreams in the African Literature*, quotes Harold W. Turner: "Are the Biblical and African worlds merely primitive, as compared with ourselves? Or is it rather that the Bible is indeed a 'book for all cultures,' and that in its ceasing to speak to our [Western] culture . . . we learn more about ourselves than we do about our Scriptures?"

God's voice does come to us in our dreams, but our dreams can also be outworkings of our own mind or even attacks from the devil. The enemy can attack us in our dreams, usually using either temptation or terror. God's voice never sounds like temptation nor terror. Martin Luther prayed over his sleep and dreams nightly: "[Heavenly Father,] graciously keep me this night. For into your hands I commend myself, my body and soul, and all things. Let your holy angel be with me, that the evil foe may have no power over me. Amen."

During a stretch of nightmares, I began praying this prayer of Luther as my last words before sleep, and after only a few nights the nightmares stopped altogether. I can't say whether my nightmares were attacks that needed the guarding of an angel, or if they were simply internal anxieties that needed to be committed to God so my subconscious didn't keep rolling them around. Either way, the nightmares clearly put my fear on display, and only prayer—along with others praying for me—helped them to go away.

Visions are like dreams but also uniquely different. Traditionally it's been understood that visions happen while you are awake and dreams happen while you are sleeping, although some believe the line is less clear.

Visions most commonly occur during prayer, but they can also appear out of nowhere. It is common to start to envision something or for an image to come to mind as you are praying. Sometimes it is an involuntary act of our own imagination, but many times it is a gift from God. I was once praying very seriously for a retreat team I was leading. I was interceding for each woman by name, and I prayed that we would all lock arms and work together for the benefit of every woman who would be coming. I saw a row of women, like dark shadows, linking arms even though I hadn't consciously thought about that image. The shadows took on a life of their own, and the shadow in the center pulled forward making a sort of V-shape. Suddenly there were many more shadows in the formation, but they were no longer women. The shadows had become birds and flew away. I took this vision as reassurance from God that all of our prayer, all of our work, all of our love would lead many women into freedom and a closer relationship with Him.

I continued to pray and ponder the image, wondering if I had conjured it up myself. But it had a weight and an element of surprise that seemed to be from the Lord. I shared my vision with another woman in leadership who had also been fervently praying, and she felt it was in line with how the Lord had been speaking to her. The weekend confirmed that the vision was from the Lord: so many tears and joyful smiles and sweet notes told us how women had experienced a new level of freedom. Instead of taking pride in our success, we took those affirmations just as we had received the image of the birds: as a gracious gift from God.

And these gifts can be promises or affirmations, but visions can also be directional signposts. Visions aren't set in stone; they aren't certain predictions of the future. Sometimes a vision of something will take a person a certain direction, and God has already planned to change that direction once she begins moving. Many times visions are assurances or affirmations for the present that get us heading in the right direction.

Also, know that having visions and dreams is not an experience exclusively for the very spiritual. Visions and dreams are just one of the many ways God reveals Himself. Sometimes He whispers, but sometimes He paints images or uses props from our daily lives.

God's voice can be any direction of our attention. Toward ourselves, toward our surroundings, or toward Him. If we let ourselves notice the brief flash in which God seems to be really present, gazing, orchestrating, and waiting, we'll learn that we are catching Him in glimmers. And those glimmers are a mere hint of His constant presence in our daily lives.

HEARING GOD'S VOICE
IN OUR DAILY LIVES

Read through these invitations to hear God speak through our daily lives. Which practice might help you listen for God's voice?

1. Choose a daily habit for this week that might help you to pay attention to the world around you. Pausing for a cup of tea? Limiting screen time? Taking a short walk? Enjoy your daily ritual for at least seven days in a row.

2. Try to notice one thing a day that reminds you of who God is or that He is near to you. Keep a journal this week.

3. Do you notice any compartmentalization in your life between "ordinary time" and "church time"? What is one way you could invite God into your daily life?

4. Have you ever had a significant experience with dreams or visions? If so, how did you process that?

CHAPTER 8

A VOICE THAT SPEAKS
IN COINCIDENCES
AND INTERRUPTIONS

The eight of us scoured the room for clues, running our palms across the walls and turning over furniture. When you walk into a room of an escape game, you have to find the questions before you find the answers. It's easy to see there are some locks that need to be opened and strange codes that need to be cracked, but nothing comes with directions. We had thirteen minutes left to unlock the door if we wanted our picture to hang on the corkboard in the lobby. Everyone was determined to claim the giant "I escaped" photo prop from the teenagers in front. In these types of immersive puzzles, it's easy not to realize something is important or to get distracted by things that seem important but have no significance. The only way to know if an answer matches a problem is when the code unlocks the door.

We all live in an immersive puzzle with no directions. Our attention gives significance to the things we notice. When we notice patterns, we decide if they are meaningful. If our discovery unlocks something interesting, we know we are onto something. Coincidences and interruptions mark moments in our lives that feel important to the puzzle. Some are accidental, and some are wondrous. Mathematical probability and spiritual significance tug at these moments, pulling hard in opposite directions, and we feel that tension. The invitation to wonder whether something is meaningful is often whispered by a divine voice. The still small whisper that lingers after the fireworks of a fantastic coincidence or a bizarre interruption.

> Flowers and birds aren't profoundly comforting in the face of unemployment, infertility, or *hereditary brain cancer*. . . . Jesus said that if we look at the birds and flowers, we'll understand how to trust God in the face of our anxiety.

Like the time God sent me flowers.

I had been getting ready for a very different Thanksgiving. Our car was half packed, and the fridge was too full. Coolers and piles of things that hadn't found a suitcase yet led to the front door like giant bread crumbs. A headache set in and slowly got worse. I set my to-do list aside and went to bed. I could finish in the morning.

My friends had tried to describe a migraine to me before, but it was hard to imagine. Their words came flooding back to me in the dark. It was the worst pain of my life. I curled up in the fetal position, afraid to move. As the dark sky turned to a slightly lighter blue, I woke my husband.

He drove all four of us—wild haired, pajama clad, and hungry— to the closest hospital. My eyes winced shut. *When did the dawn become so unbearable?* The nurse took us straight back to a darkened room. I explained that I was having a migraine.

"Oh," said the doctor calmly, when she came in. "I see you have a history of brain cancer in your family."

I don't usually forget that my dad died ten weeks before my wedding day or that my sister-in-law is a living miracle.

"I'd like to see a CAT scan," said the doctor, "so that we can rule out anything more serious."

Gently, the thought floated in: *Just breathe.*

Those two words were on a slide in my PowerPoint deck titled "Choose Worship Instead of Worry." I had taught this idea many times before. Once I even counted down to help an entire congregation take a deep breath together. All the words of Jesus, memorized Scripture, and hours of prayer came back to me as I coached my body to breathe deeply in a slow, steady rhythm. In . . . and out. . . .

I clicked through my slide deck in my mind. Jesus tells us not to worry. He says that if we focus on the kingdom of God, then the rest of life's logistics work out (Matthew 6:25–33). He proves His point with two examples: the birds and the wildflowers.

Flowers and birds aren't profoundly comforting in the face of unemployment, infertility, or *hereditary brain cancer*. It would be easy to shuffle this sappy sound bite of Jesus to the side and look for something more helpful. But it would be a mistake. Jesus said that if we look at the birds and flowers, we'll understand how to trust God in the face of our anxiety. Hundreds of years earlier, God told Job that if he looked at the ravens, he would know how to trust in the face of pain (Job 38:41). As strange as it sounds, these birds and flowers must mean something.

As I sat there, I remembered I had spent all spring and summer that year staring at flowers and watching birds. God provides food for the birds, and they seem to start each day singing in joyful anticipation. Wildflowers are . . . wild. They grow in the absolutely most ridiculous places. These unexpected, undervalued, overlooked bursts of color are in every grocery store parking lot and underfoot in every grassy field. Beauty recklessly wasted yet always breaking through.

The birds showed me I could wake up knowing that God is good, and unafraid of each new day. The flowers brightly proclaimed that God is everywhere and that His beautiful fingerprints are on every surface no matter how ugly, dry, or broken.

I knew better than to worry. I knew to have faith. But that knowledge wasn't helping. I couldn't even pray. I could barely breathe, but that's all I had. Breathing in, I recited, "There is pain in the night." Breathing out, I recited, "But joy comes in the morning" (Psalm 30:5). In . . . and out . . . the prayer of breath. . . . My faith felt so weak. *God, I should have more faith than this.*

There were no scan technicians in the office so early on Thanksgiving morning. The hospital staff needed to call someone in, and the wait could be a couple of hours. My toddlers were perched on the side of my bed. My youngest was nuzzling his face into my legs through the stiff hospital blanket. My husband stepped into the hall to make plans for our kids. He leaned his head through the doorway after he put his phone back in his pocket.

"I'll be right back. Are you going to be okay?"

I nodded.

"You *are* going to be okay," he reassured.

As he disappeared, a tear rolled down my cheek. My headache finally responding to the IV, I glanced at my phone and noticed a text from a friend: "I don't want to bug you if you are resting, but I'm praying for you. Call me if you want to pray." I called. I told her I was scared, but also strangely peaceful. The peace actually scared me a little. *Was that something dying people had?* I told her I was hoping the technician could come soon and I could be home for Thanksgiving dinner. I wanted a migraine, not a brain tumor. My friend started praying, first for the tech to come quickly and then for—

We were interrupted by a knock at my door. The technician who was supposed to take hours to arrive had come within twenty minutes. He helped me get into a wheelchair and guided me down the hall to a large room with wires and lights in every corner and a daunting chamber in the center. My heart started racing. I tried to pray . . . but I couldn't. I tried to remember my friend's prayer . . . but to no avail. My rib cage tightened. The technician gave me some instructions and helped me lean back and lie on the sliding platform.

That's when I looked up.

The ceiling was covered by a mural of wildflowers.

Of all the hospitals near our home, of all the CAT scan machines, of all the art . . . of course God had brought me here! I laughed out loud. Jesus's voice carried from Matthew 6 again, telling me not to worry. I paused and noticed all the wildflower beauty of my morning. Getting in to see the doctor with no wait, a doctor who cared enough to look at my files, friends who were caring for my kids, friends who were texting me and praying for me, prayers answered before they were even finished.

As I lay in the tube with the buzzing and clicking all around my skull, my muscles softened. My heart rate slowed. I could finally pray. *My faith doesn't have to be enough. Your goodness is always enough. Thank You.*

The doctor knocked on the door a little while later. "It's not uncommon for women of a certain age to begin developing migraines," she said, flipping through a clipboard of paper. "Your brain scan came back unremarkable. You are free to go."

As if my life hadn't hung in the balance moments before, she and her long white coat turned and walked out the door to her next patient. *False alarm.* As happy as I was to walk out of the hospital that afternoon with my unremarkable brain, I was even more thankful for all the remarkable "coincidences" that showed me God was with me all morning, not just in the test results.

People who have experienced powerful coincidences are more likely to notice more coincidences. Religious, intuitive, self-referential, optimistic, and meaning-seeking people are also more likely to notice a coincidence.

A coincidence can be any connection of events that is not easily explained, and those occurrences tend to spark wonder or excitement. Scientists and saints alike are fascinated by coincidences, but the two groups think about them very differently.

What, for instance, are the odds of my seeing a flower on the ceiling right when I most need to be reminded of God's goodness? A scientific thinker would say the likelihood was pretty high. Considering the lack of specificity, the odds were in my favor. It could have been an image of a flower or a real flower, it didn't need to be a specific kind of flower, and flowers are a common item around hospitals. My miracle coincidence could easily be understood as an example of the Law of Truly Large Numbers: with a large enough sample, any outrageous thing is likely to happen.

Arnold M. Zwicky, a linguistics professor at Stanford University, adds the Frequency Illusion as another scientific lens for coincidences. He first explains that when we see or notice something that interests us, we tend to notice it again more easily. You've experienced this before. That time you were thinking of taking a vacation somewhere, or buying a certain car, or saw someone wearing something interesting, and then you started to see or hear things related to that over and over. The second component of the Frequency Illusion is confirmation bias. Once we feel like we have made sense of something, our brain is hesitant to let our certainty go. According to the Frequency Illusion, if you notice that all the high schoolers at the mall are wearing short shorts, then you will notice short shorts everywhere. You may also stop seeing all the teens who are wearing anything other than short shorts.

A psychiatry professor at the University of Virginia, Bernard D. Beitman, MD, published a paper on coincidences in the *Psychiatric Annals*. There he noted that certain types of people are more likely to notice connections and coincidences. People, for instance, notice coincidences more often when they are in a heightened emotional state like sadness, anger, or anxiety. People who have experienced powerful coincidences are more likely to notice more coincidences. Religious, intuitive, self-referential, optimistic, and meaning-seeking people are also more likely to notice a coincidence.

In a heightened emotional state of anxiety, then, a religious person like me who had been studying common wildflowers for months was almost guaranteed to coincidentally see a flower and find meaning in it. The Law of Truly Large Numbers, the Frequency Illusion, and Psychiatry 101 are all at play. So why did it feel so acutely like a reassurance from God?

For all the scientific theory, coincidences are surprisingly difficult to study using the scientific method of observation, measurement, and experiment. This methodology involves the formulation, testing, and subsequent modification of a hypothesis.

Coincidences are rarely reproducible, and many of the elements of a coincidence are hearsay. No one can prove that she was thinking about someone the moment that person called. And no one can prove that he had a dream about the same blue car with dice hanging in the window that he saw the next day. Or that I was thinking about wildflowers when I was taken to Exam Room 3.

In *Mere Christianity*, C. S. Lewis postulates, "Supposing science ever became complete so that it knew every single thing in the whole universe. Is it not plain that the questions, 'Why is there a universe?' 'Why does it go on as it does?' 'Has it any meaning?' would remain just as they were?"

The question "What does a coincidence mean?" is not a scientific question. Any attempt to boil a coincidence down to scientific theory will not only fail to answer the question of meaning, but it will also miss the essence of the event entirely. Think about the greatest love story you know or the most in love you have ever been. Now, imagine someone in a lab coat retelling that story by describing only brain chemistry, environmental factors, and physical health. The science may be accurate, but it will miss the love story entirely.

There are other psychologists, like Carl Jung, who believe that coincidences are signs of the interconnectedness in our world. Jung coined the term "synchronicity" to describe awe-inspiring coincidences and connections. Jung is only one of many scientists, artists, and observers to notice the significance of coincidences. Synchronistic thinkers have many theories about what causes coincidences. Some believe coincidences happen because of the physical connectedness of our universe, or because of a secret language of the natural world, or as sign of divine involvement. The one thing these theories all have in common is a fascination with the way reality occasionally veers from the script. I'm with those who desire to wonder at the wrinkles in our world instead of iron them out.

Some synchronistic insight, however, sounds more like New Age philosophy than Christian wisdom. They sense that coincidences have some spiritual significance, but any explanation of spirituality apart from God can quickly morph into strange theories. Like the people the apostle Paul encountered who worshipped an "unknown God," these synchronistic thinkers recognize a truth that they don't yet understand.

The stories of Jesus show God speaking through coincidences, though we miss a lot of them because we don't understand the history and culture. When Jesus multiplied bread and fish, He "coincidentally" left behind twelve baskets of leftovers—and that's more than a lot of leftovers. *Twelve!* That number would register with any Jew as the number of the tribes of Judah. Could this be the Messiah who provides for His people?

Coincidences tell us the story of a God we all know. Our God who created order out of desolate nothingness. The great Mathematician and Artist who designed the night and day like clockwork but refused to create humans to be predictable robots. A rational Risk-Taker. God lives in the tension we feel between predictable order and unfathomable anomaly, inviting His children to both understand the natural world and be humbled by the mystery of our supernatural reality.

God speaks through coincidences. We should pay attention, but be wise before we speculate. Not everything that is exciting is important. Isn't it fun when you discover you share a birthday with someone? If you stand in a room with twenty-two other people, there is a 50 percent chance that two people in that room will have the same birthday. If you add another fifty-two people, you get to a 99.9 percent chance. Choosing the man you are going to marry because he has the same birthday as your grandpa may not be the word from God you thought you were hearing. Just as science cannot rule out that some coincidences have meaning, faith cannot determine that every coincidence does.

Coincidences can also be God's answer to prayer. Francis Chan tells of preparing for a project to feed the homeless in San Francisco. They realized the day before that they were not going to have enough food. He confidently told his team that God would provide, but then he closed his door, prayed, and cried. Hours before the event the next morning, his team got a call from a local grocery store. The store was experiencing a power outage and asked if they could donate all the food from their refrigerators.

Coincidences are just as often an invitation to prayer as they are an answer. There is an opportunity to explore the significance of the situation and to ask God how we should respond. When we ask God what He means by these circumstances instead of assuming we know, we can find the wisdom or confirmation that we need.

I visit inmates in our local jail as a volunteer chaplain. Recently I sat with a woman whose mother had died while she was incarcerated. Like many of the women I've visited, she had a family member who had taken her to church as a kid, but she didn't remember much. She also hadn't thought about God for a long time. That had recently changed. She had been crying on her bed for hours after she found out her mom passed away. Her mom had been sick for a long time, and the inmate was convinced that being sent to jail, and the accusations that were made against her, caused her mom to decline quickly. She blamed herself for her mom's death. When this grieving woman had no more breath or tears, she stared out the one small window in her cell and noticed how blue the sky was. Just then a white bird flew by.

"Is that You, God?" She was surprised to hear her own voice ask the question aloud.

> Coincidences are just as often an invitation to prayer as they are an answer. There is an opportunity to explore the significance of the situation and to ask God how we should respond.

The next day, having heard about her mother, another chaplain came to visit. The chaplain told her, "I've come to offer you peace and comfort from God, who loves you." The chaplain reached into her bag and pulled out a book for her. On the cover was a white dove against a perfectly blue sky.

"Do you think that was God speaking to me?" the inmate asked me. "It felt like maybe God was telling me that He is here with me. In jail and in my pain."

I told her it sure sounded like something God would say. "Let's pray and ask Him," I said. "I know that God promises to be with us, and the Bible says God is close to people with broken hearts. Jesus told us that we can know God is good when we look at the flowers and the birds. God has sent me flowers before. I bet He sends birds too."

God sends so many surprises our way. If coincidences are wrinkles in our world that spark wonder, interruptions are the more irritating version of reality going off script. Interruptions come as invasions of our plans, dreams, productivity, and sometimes our identity. The magic of coincidences is something we can muse over while plucking petals from a daisy, but interruptions don't engage our wonder for long before annoyance, anger, or blame join the party. But God's words and wisdom can come to us through interruptions if we are paying attention.

I almost pee my pants all the time. It's my ridiculous rebellion against interruption. Since I was a little girl and all the way to being my adult self, I have hated the need to stop what I am doing to go to the bathroom. Just one more time down the slide. Just one more e-mail to send. When I am on a roll, I cannot stand being interrupted, even by my own body.

You can imagine how motherhood has messed with me. My sweet babies started by interrupting my sleep, then they interrupted my career, and now they interrupt me a thousand times a day. Interruptions have knocked me out of my rhythm again and again. Sometimes they invite me to be present in the moment, but sometimes they make me want to scream.

Interruptions come in all shapes and sizes, from minor inconveniences to life-altering events. After all, change is the only constant in our world, but its frequency does not make it any less annoying or even terrifying. When the marriage that was supposed to last forever ends, when the person who should be alive dies, when the baby who was supposed to be a part of your family isn't, when the job that was providing for your family disappears, when the dream that felt within reach vanishes—these interruptions are jolting in the deepest parts of who we are.

As John Ortberg observes in his book *God Is Closer than You Think*, "It is possible that what we see as an inconvenient interruption is a divine appointment." God is famous for His interruptions. Think about Abraham, Noah, Joseph, Moses, Rahab, Jonah, Gideon, Esther, Job, Mary, every disciple of Jesus, the apostle Paul . . . actually, this is going to be a problem. I'm struggling to think of a notable person in the Bible whose life *wasn't* interrupted by God.

When God breaks into our stories or leads us on an unexpected detour, it's rarely painless. The Joseph of rainbow-coat fame had his sweet life as favorite son interrupted to be sold into slavery by his own brothers and later wrongfully convicted and sentenced to prison. Mary the mother of Jesus should have had an uneventful engagement, but she surrendered her reputation to the interruption of an angel, and Mary would one day watch her Son of God die on a cross. The apostle Paul had his reign of power and influence interrupted to be blinded, beaten, imprisoned, shipwrecked, and tortured to the brink of death.

So if we are walking in the footsteps of Jesus, we shouldn't be surprised if we come to a cross. When that happens, do not be afraid. That's not where Christ's footsteps end. We follow Him to a tomb, and He holds our hand through the resurrection. Joseph went from being a selfish youngest child to being a ruler of Egypt and savior of Israel. Mary was destined for a mediocre life in an obscure town before she became the woman who nursed God in the flesh. Saul was an enemy of Christ who became Paul, a key leader in establishing the Christian church. Even with too many scars to count, Paul called his prior life of comfort and achievement absolute garbage.

Jesus says if we want a new life, we have to lose our old one (Matthew 16:25).

In his classic *Mere Christianity*, C. S. Lewis quotes the insight of George MacDonald:

> Imagine yourself as a living house. God comes in to rebuild that house. At first, perhaps, you can understand what He is doing. He is getting the drains right and stopping the leaks in the roof and so on; you knew that those jobs needed doing and so you are not surprised. But presently He starts knocking the house about in a way that hurts abominably and does not seem to make any sense. What on earth is He up to? The explanation is that He is building quite a different house from the one you thought of—throwing out a new wing here, putting on an extra floor there, running up towers, making courtyards. You thought you were being made into a decent little cottage: but He is building a palace. He intends to come and live in it Himself.

Do not forget that God has known you from before your earliest beginning, when you were still a dream of His. He created you and gave you gifts, talents, and reflections of Himself that you uniquely show to the world. When God interrupts our lives, He is often doing more than leading us back to Him. In bringing us closer to a right relationship with Him, God is also bringing us back to His original design of who we are. We will never find our truest identity when we are defining ourselves by what we have, what we can do, or who loves us. Interruptions to the false narrative of who we are or what will make us happy are painful gifts. God wants infinitely more *for* us than He wants to take *from* us. Your life isn't being ripped out from under you; a new life is being offered to you.

Losing my dad, losing my overleveraged town house, and losing my job were painful interruptions to a life that I liked a lot. In the end, those losses meant gaining a new life of spiritual freedom, financial freedom, and discovering new dreams. Dreams that had more to do with what I loved than with what I thought would impress people.

I've learned to trust God's interruptions in the big things. He's taken me on so many twists and turns that turned out better than I could imagine, I'm actually learning to enjoy the ride. For some reason, it's almost harder to accept His interruptions in my daily life. Losing precious time or paying money for things I wasn't expecting doesn't feel like gaining new life at all. Still, the neighbor girl who swings by because I always have apples and peanut butter or my child who wants to sit in my lap while I'm trying to read can all lead me to the woman I was meant to be.

It is humbling to be interrupted. Interruptions not only point

> God wants infinitely more *for* us than He wants to take *from* us. . . . I've learned to trust God's interruptions in the big things. He's taken me on so many twists and turns that turned out better than I could imagine, I'm actually learning to enjoy the ride.

out our own limitations of control, they also require us to put other people's needs before our own. They push us to serve the friend who always needs to talk or the kid who forever wants a glass of water even when we'd rather not be bothered. Interruptions also demand Sabbath, the ability to step away from work and let it be good enough for now. There is no surrender like the willingness to be interrupted.

My friend Andy is a pastor and a rock star. Literally, a rock star. He has been all over the world leading worship in crowded arenas and at giant music festivals. One night he was driving home after his band played for the biggest crowd he'd ever been on stage for. He was still soaking it all in . . . adrenaline rushing . . . prayers and worship flowing out of him as he passed the streetlights . . . full of energy and completely exhausted at the same time.

As Andy was praying, he noticed a homeless man on a corner and felt a strong urge to go talk to him. He continued to worship as he drove, but he sensed God wanted something other than a song or a prayer. Andy was supposed to go talk to that man. It wasn't too late to turn back, but he kept driving home. He was tired. He had already poured himself out in service to God that night, and he had nothing left. He was done. The rest of his drive home, he sat in guilty silence.

Days later, when the excuses and justifications collapsed, Andy wished he could go back in time. He couldn't believe that after offering God the greatest night of worship he could imagine, with thousands of people joining his voice, he then failed to honor God in the quiet of his drive home. Andy still tells the story of that night as a time God taught him about true worship. Worship is not just telling God that He is King. Real worship is putting down our cell phones, closing our laptops, setting an alarm, or even pulling our car over in acknowledgment that God's agenda is more important than our own. True worship is being willing to be interrupted.

St. Therese of Lisieux (1873–97) lived under the strict order of a Carmelite community where she had little discretionary time to herself. She lived with the daily frustration of not being as productive or as creative as she had hoped, a frustration I know well. Everything changed when she started praying the same prayer before the small window of time she had each day opened. "I choose to be interrupted," she would whisper to God. She listened for His whispers back, taking each interruption as it came. Sometimes as an assignment from God. Sometimes as a stretch for her to trust His provision or timing. She graciously accepted each ordinary interruption. When she was not interrupted, she would thank God. When she was interrupted, she would thank God.

When I wake up in the dark of morning now and a raggle-taggle pajama monkey gets out of bed too early, I set my Bible down. I know my time with God is not meant for being frustrated that I didn't finish a psalm. I hold my baby close and breathe in the smell of his hair. I think about the love God has as a Parent and how often He lets me interrupt Him even though He is King of heaven. I pray. And I start with "I choose to be interrupted."

HEARING GOD'S VOICE IN COINCIDENCES AND INTERRUPTIONS

Read through these invitations to hear God speak through coincidences and interruptions. Which practice might help you listen for God's voice?

1. Is there a "coincidence" in which you have been able to notice God's hand in? Pray and ask Him to show you.

2. Keep a journal of times when God seems to draw your attention to a coincidence in your life. Pray about what you notice, and keep track of ways in which the coincidences either are confirmed or seem to lose their significance. Talk with a mentor or friend about what you are hearing, and explore what God might be saying to you right now.

3. When, if ever, have you seen God shape your character? What have those experiences been like? In what ways have you changed as a result?

4. Choose a daily time to pray "I choose to be interrupted" as a prayer of humility, Sabbath, and surrender. Look for ways God may be redirecting you through His interruptions. Even if it is unclear how God is working, thank Him for the ways He is both deconstructing and rebuilding your life during this season.

CHAPTER 9

A VOICE THAT SPEAKS IN BEAUTY ALL AROUND US

As our car wound up the rocky dirt cross-backs, it occurred to me that we should have driven something with four-wheel drive. The tree cover was so dense that the sunlight only shot through the leaves in slender, sharp blades that briefly cut through the dust clouds. We had chosen a "secret ridge"—first come, first served—to camp at that night. We snaked through the turns that were scribbled in pink ink on our hand-drawn map. Turns out, this place was not such a secret after all. Every flat space large enough for a tent and a car was occupied: by a bachelor party, by a homeless man, and by a couple who adamantly waved us away. The fog began rolling in, and the blades of sunlight gave way to a ubiquitous hazy gray light. It would be dark soon, we were in the middle of nowhere, and we needed to make camp. The excitement of loading up the gear for our girls' weekend was fading as we debated which of the strangers we should ask to share their campsite.

Just as the three of us girls were getting ready to crash the angry honeymooners' site, we glanced at a small clearing off the other side of the road. It was right on the edge of the cliff, and there wasn't much space, but we could pull the car in. The fog was thick as we set up our tent. Our winter hats and gloves were coming in handy. We needed to make a fire. This little patch of dirt wasn't much, but it would have to do. The fog began thinning, and through the gray-striped sky—to our amazement—a deep rose-orange was blushing through. We were mesmerized by the shapes and colors that were emerging behind the disappearing clouds.

"Look! It's the ocean!"

The perch on which we had nested was something like a ship's crow's nest, spying heaven as it broke through to earth. We could see the entire panorama of the mountains flowing down in lush valleys, like the train of its emerald evening gown casually graced the coast below. The rocky cliffs were not at war with the waves now. The water had given up crashing for the moment. Along with us, the ocean was stunned into stillness watching the giant orange sun dip toward the horizon. Had the blazing ball of light not set fire to the top of the water as it came nearer, we would have never known where the sky stopped and the ocean began.

Our faces, like the sky, glowed. My eyes welled up in awe as my breath quickened. I wonder what sunset David was watching when he wrote this:

The heavens declare the glory of God;
  the skies proclaim the work of his hands.
Day after day they pour forth speech;
  night after night they reveal knowledge.

They have no speech, they use no words;
>   no sound is heard from them.
Yet their voice goes out into all the earth,
>   their words to the ends of the world. (Psalm 19:1–4)

Nature uses no words, but speaks loudly. It's one of the many voices that can tell us who God is and point us toward His goodness. When we cannot imagine God's goodness, when we struggle to believe He is real, the sky is there to shout, "Glory!" The sun rising and setting, the stars strung in a canopy above us at night—their witness to God covers us when we need it most.

The whole of Scripture wraps us in a dramatic plot of rebellion and radical redemption, and with so many characters and plot twists it's easy to forget how the story began. Before everything was undone, life started the way God intended—in a beautiful garden. Echoes of God's walking presence, the perfect relationship and connection of all things, and the overwhelming beauty of unpolluted creation haunt us. The first tabernacle was designed with the imagery of the garden of Eden. God gifted artisans to create beautiful metalwork and hewn gems. He knows the effect of art. He knew how art could call His people to a garden they'd never visited before and conjure emotions of homesickness and loss and hope. God gifted musicians for the temple, because music fills heaven, and He knows that the beauty of a voice or an instrument can unify us and awaken our spirit in surprising ways. Even in our polluted world, the beauty and design of nature speaks powerfully of the goodness and order of God.

If the beauty of nature draws us toward God, we shouldn't be surprised that Scripture often calls our attention to nature.

The Bible is full of nature images that illustrate God's care, His timing, and His plan. The seasons are such a powerful metaphor for change, someone could wonder if God created them with a plan to teach us His wisdom for navigating the constant flow of change in our own lives.

> There is a time for everything,
> and a season for every activity under the heavens.
> (Ecclesiastes 3:1)

The teacher in Ecclesiastes used his metaphor of the seasons to talk for fourteen couplets about the seasons in a human's life: times of living and dying, planting and harvesting, crying and laughing, and being quiet and speaking up. The seasons have so much to say about change, and God has so much to say to us through the seasons.

Seasons remind us to *expect change*, and God whispers, "Your right now is not your forever."

There will always be death, and there will always be life. The trees and seasons are more comfortable with that dance: they try to remind us not to be afraid of shedding our leaves.

A fig tree in our backyard fans its giant green leaves to form the most gorgeous canopy in the summer. We moved our patio table right below it, not caring if the fruit drops and splatters there. It is winter now, and our summer tree is barely recognizable. There are no leaves, and we can see straight through to the neighbor's yard.

As I look at those tall standing twigs, it seems a miracle that the same tree can experience life and death so many times, year after year. When I am experiencing the death of my identity, of friendships, of dreams, I find a God-promise in my fig tree. The bare branches call out, "It's winter, but spring is coming." Trees lose their leaves for many reasons: to conserve water when it is scarce, to resist the weight of snow that could catch on those leaves and break the branches, and to make room for new growth. God says sometimes He is the One who prunes back our leaves for those same purposes: "He prunes to make [the branch] even more fruitful" (John 15:2 BSB).

Whatever death we are grieving now, that death may be permanent. Leaves fall and are raked away, and autumn burn piles fill the air with a strangely sweet and acrid smoke. If we only see the smoke rise, we could sit in despair forever. If we lift our eyes to the trees, we find our hope. As time passes, seasons change: the tree itself has not died as its leaves did. New life is coming. It will never be quite the same, but new leaves that reach higher than the ones the year before arrive every spring. New figs will drop onto the patio, making chores for sticky little hands and food for sneaky little squirrels. There will always be death, and there will always be life. The trees and seasons are more comfortable with that dance: they try to remind us not to be afraid of shedding our leaves.

Seasons remind us that *change is full of contradictions*, and God whispers, "Look around . . . there are surprises everywhere."

I can be too quick to name the season I'm in, and I can too easily forget that seasonal change means constant fluctuation. When I had a newborn, I thought my season of being a new mom was the defining and all-encompassing rhythm of my life. I forgot about spring. Seasons aren't neat and tidy: they don't abruptly or completely turn with the solstice of the moon. In late March, for instance, I walked in the woods looking for spring. The smell was there, and the bright green sprouts were emerging low to the ground. It was a sunny spring day, but the banks of the flowing creek still had chunks of ice and a frosting of snow in the shaded parts. Either winter was still fighting for its hold, or spring is not threatened by a little snow. I think it might be both. Just because we are grieving doesn't mean a little laughter can't sneak in. When we should be the happiest in our lives and all is going well, it's okay for the icy snow of pain to linger in the shade. It's normal. Just ask the creek. It will tell you.

Seasons remind us that *change is not universal*, and God whispers, "Love one another."

Later that spring, closer to home, summer was on the move. The sun was changing from bright to warm, and my skin was tingling with UV rays. For the first time in ages, I drove down the road with my windows down as some startling news poured out my radio: Blizzards strike with record snowfall on the East Coast! School cancelled! Elderly in danger! Roads dangerous! It was the strangest thing to hear on national news that we were experiencing the coldest spring in decades as my hair was warming in the California sun. Just because it is April everywhere does not mean we are all living in the same season.

After my dad's funeral, for instance, I watched in amazement as the rest of the world moved on. I felt like the freak East Coast snowstorm with my blizzard hanging over my head in summertime. I wanted to hide. Fortunately my friends weren't afraid to get cold or wet, however inconvenient or unnecessary it was for them to meet me under my cloud. They understood Romans 12:

part of being the family of God is weeping with those who weep (v. 15). I learned, too, that I could step out from under my cloud, however difficult that may be, and also live out this verse. I could still celebrate with my friends who were getting engaged and being promoted at work. We're all in our different seasons, but every season is better when we share the experience with each other.

Seasons remind us that *change happens slowly*, and God whispers, "Be patient."

As much as seasons fluctuate and overlap, they are never hurried. They speak God's patience and timing to us. We live in a crazy internet world where we can get almost anything from anywhere within a few shipping days. Anything, anytime. We forget that life cycles in nature rarely involve instant results. Our earth teaches us that seeds need to be planted, nourished, and given time to grow. Acorns don't become oak trees in a microwave. Instead, they spend years underground and invisible. Then they become barely noticeable as a seedling. As we observe God's design for the strong oak tree, we shouldn't expect our own dreams to wildly succeed overnight. After all, God is nurturing us and growing us in our seasons. There is no fast-forward button.

In the slowness of my own seasons, my life can feel like a planter box full of dirt with no seedlings in sight. Then I remember that God is growing my character and increasing my opportunities in ways I cannot see. Before the flower blooms, the tomato ripens, or the tree gives shade, the miracle of birth and growth happens in the darkness underground. It amazes me to think of how God tends to His wildest rainforest gardens and how He cares for me as well. The seasons comfort me as I wait, as I grow. I know that when it seems like nothing is happening, something *is* happening.

Finally, seasons remind us that *God is good*, and He whispers, "I think you're going to like this."

God gives us the seasons not only as a witness to His design and process, but also as a pure gift. In *The Screwtape Letters*, C. S. Lewis animates a demon who complains about God's goodness in the seasons:

> He has contrived to gratify both tastes together in the very world He has made, by that union of change and permanence which we call Rhythm. He gives them the seasons, each season different yet every year the same, so that spring is always felt as a novelty yet always as the recurrence of an immemorial theme.

The world can feel overcome by evil, but coming closer to nature we remember that God's goodness still surrounds us. Nature isn't just a metaphor for God's ways and designs, it can be a meeting place with God Himself.

Although I'm not always sure if I'm an introvert or an extrovert, I know I am only now beginning to be comfortable in solitude, alone with myself. The closer we get to the earth, the fewer places there are to run from our thoughts and fears. There's no shopping, junk food, alcohol, electronic screens, or constant busyness to numb my pain or to keep me from noticing I'm still insecure, still selfish, still controlling, and still chasing satisfaction from things that can never make me happy. I took Nouwen's book on solitude, *The Way of the Heart*, into the wilderness, read it atop a mossy log, and cried. On those pages he describes the solitude I most strongly feel surrounded by nature:

Solitude is the furnace of transformation. . . . Solitude is the place of the great struggle and the great encounter— the struggle against the compulsions of the false self, and the encounter with the loving God who offers himself as the substance of the new self.

Of course we can meet God anywhere: His voice speaks into our lives in extraordinary places of natural beauty as well as in towering skyscrapers. Still, there is nothing like the wilderness to call us into aloneness with God. When we are alone in creation, we are surrounded by testimonies of God's care, His design, His history, and His goodness. Out in the natural world, we are small and overwhelmed, yet there we can meet God alone. Stripped of our devices to assure us we are okay, we can face our darkest fears, allow ourselves to not be okay, and fall into the truth we knew was always there: we, too, are God's creation, broken and beloved.

> Because we are created in God's image, we carry both the image of our Creator and the image of being a creator. When we create opportunities, art, safe space, food, music, roads, or technology, we are doing the equivalent of Adam and Eve's gardening.

Because we are created in God's image, we carry both the image of our Creator and the image of being a creator.

When we create opportunities, art, safe space, food, music, roads, or technology, we are doing the equivalent of Adam and Eve's gardening. We are calming the chaos, we are stewarding resources, we are taking care of the earth and one another.

Creation is not limited to art, but art has a unique role in creation. Poetry, paintings, music, sculptures, and stories can capture our imagination. They can bring us closer to something beautiful or something sad than we would have ever ventured on our own. Art ties threads of connection through the human experience. As we listen to a song or as we stare at a painting, art makes us feel something that we would not have otherwise felt.

I had my first profound experience with art after I graduated from college. My dad gave me his frequent flyer miles so I could fly to Europe and backpack from London to Rome with my best friend. The saturation of art was almost overwhelming as she and I went to the most incredible museums during the day before we crashed in the cheapest hostels at night. I'll never forget our visit to the Musée d'Orsay.

We had already been awed by the Louvre the day before, but now we wandered the vaulted and well-lit d'Orsay. The ceilings were so tall that some paintings were hung above others, very high up. A Nikolai Nikolaevich Ge hung almost at the ceiling, and I had to crane my head far back to see. In my low place, staring high up, I was transfixed by *The Crucifixion on Golgotha*, painted in 1893.

The only images of crosses I had grown up with were simple, looking like a lowercase *t*. They hung in glittering silver around women's necks, or they were the background to a photo set against a picturesque sky. Never had I seen a cross like this. Never had I seen Jesus's face in such agony. Never had I felt so enraged at this injustice, so shamed by my sin, so loved by God, and so completely forgiven. My eyes welled with tears of love and gratitude that no sermon could have evoked. Art has a sacred place in communicating the truth of God.

When we create art, it doesn't have to be a painting of a religious subject to be deeply spiritual. As long as the art is excellent, a picture of a refugee child receiving water or a poem about the heartbreak of losing a child equally draw us to listen, to see God and to see one another. May God speak to us as we create, drawing our attention to the details and whisper the beauty He longs for us to see and to show others. May we create more than just an image *of* God's glory. May we create *as* God's image and *to* His glory.

The beauty all around us in nature and in art can call our attention to God's good character, His heart as a Creator, and the things He longs to tell us about our world and ourselves. A natural response to that revelation of beauty is a heart of worship. Worship takes many forms, but it is always a posture of elevating God above ourselves.

Worship is our expression of love and desire. We are wired to worship. We all worship something, whether we realize it or not. No wonder so much of the Old Testament calls God's people out of idolatry and so much of the New Testament is focused on calling God's people to Jesus. Jesus said that if we want to follow God, we can't set our hearts on anything else:

> Lay up for yourselves treasures in heaven, where neither moth nor rust destroys and where thieves do not break in and steal. For where your treasure is, there your heart will be also. . . . You cannot serve God and money. (Matthew 6:20–21, 24 ESV)

We are all putting our treasure somewhere. Our precious time, our hard-earned money, our limited relational energy—all are being invested. Where they go, there goes our heart. There goes our allegiance. There goes our worship.

Worship isn't just complimenting God; it's wanting God. It's acknowledging that His ways and His understanding are greater than our own—not just by saying so but by aligning the details and decisions of our lives with that truth. It's investing in our relationship with God and His way of life.

My life, simply lived loving God, is my foundational act of worship. Otherwise, without love, even the most melodic worship song is a screeching guitar and even the greatest sacrifice I make is a cringe-worthy stunt (1 Corinthians 13). Love is not just a feeling; it's a force. Love compels us to obey the wisdom and the way of Jesus (John 14:15). Love compels us to turn our feelings into action (Luke 10:27–37). Worship is an act of love, but it's also a discipline that can train us to direct our love. The habit of worshipping both individually and in community can change us.

The songs we sing may not matter as much as the heart we sing them from, but singing praise together and to one another was important in the early church: "Speaking to one another with psalms, hymns, and songs from the Spirit. Sing and make music from your heart to the Lord" (Ephesians 5:19).

Worship is not only an individual response to God, it's a source of unity and strength in Christian community. Worship calls diverse and unlikely people to the same table, where we can all remind each other of how amazing God is. Our worship is not only a gift to God; it's a gift from God, a gift we give to one another as the ministry of presence. Research has shown that face-to-face interaction lowers our cortisol (stress hormone) and raises our oxytocin (love hormone). When we make the effort to show up to church to worship together, we show up for each other.

I remember attending a large Christian event in a stadium with twenty thousand women. We were singing and worshipping together, then the band faded, and we sang a cappella. Our voices carried strong. Initially caught up in the beauty of the voices, I sang even louder until we finished the chorus, and I stood there crying. I was absolutely sure this was what heaven was like, the church worshipping God (Revelation 5:11–14), but I had never tasted it before. It was beautiful.

It amazes me that good music teaches and encourages me when I am present and engaged. I'm not a spectator; I'm participating in it. Singing truths about God and who He is shapes my feelings and my thoughts for the day, and sometimes an incredible lyric will haunt me for much longer. Just as the Holy Spirit speaks to us through the Scriptures we've memorized, God can speak to us through songs and hymns when we need them most.

God doesn't need my worship or yours. He isn't fading into the dark like Tinker Bell waiting for someone to clap for Him. It's by God's grace that we can worship. But what do we have to give or say to the God of the universe? It is not even a bad singing voice or the "right" words that God is after. He wants us. He wants us to live abundantly in the freedom and perfect design He has always dreamed for us. As Greek bishop and theologian Irenaeus (130–202) put it, "The glory of God is man fully alive."

I got a taste of feeling fully alive during a trip to the mountains with a few friends. We heard a rumor about a swimming hole with a giant, smooth rock towering over it. Candy Rock. At the right time of year, the rock has a waterfall coming down, and the small falls against the smooth rock forms something like a waterslide.

The way we hiked in, we came across Candy Rock from the top. The water below at the base of the falls looked perfectly green, but a long way down. A couple of us hiked to the bottom to gauge the depth of the water, and as I looked up to where the other girls awaited our verdict they looked so small against the brightness of the sun. This was a tall rock.

"Yep! It's deep enough," I called up.

On the hike back to the top, I had an identity crisis. A few years ago I would have been the first one to jump off that rock. . . .

Why am I so scared now? Is it because I have kids at home? Why can't I stop thinking about Joni Eareckson Tada's biography? Is this what getting older is like? Was I ever fun, or was that just me trying to impress people? Who am I?

"Jump in. Worship Me."

The words came from nowhere, but I had a very strong impression that God wanted me to jump in. For worship? That didn't make sense. Just then the idea came clearly that God wanted me to enjoy His creation, to play on the rocks He formed, and to embrace an identity He saw in me that was braver than I felt in myself. *Okay, Lord.*

"I'll go first."

Everyone backed up a few steps as I walked to the edge of the rock. I sat down carefully, not knowing what to expect from the force of the water—and I was swept away! I flew down that rock squealing with delight—what a ride!—and the force of the waterfall plunged me deep below the green water at the bottom. From the dark coldness I followed the bubbles up toward the light, where I broke through the surface of the water and took a gasping inhale of pure mountain air. I felt like I had been baptized. No longer a slave to fear, I had been born into a vision of playful bravery that I didn't have for myself.

I still remind myself of that wild, scary ride—that strange act of worship—on days when I feel too scared to try. Times when I'd rather play it safe. If God is greater than I am, I can trust Him. My acts of worship aren't just me talking to God, singing to God, making sacrifices to God: God is not a passive recipient of our worship. Worship (the right ordering of my loves and priorities and living the life God has for me) is a response to God's beauty that actually leads me to even more of His goodness. I can hear His voice. I can have fun. I can be brave. I can jump into any water He is calling me to, because He has beautiful things for me there.

I don't always know how to be fully alive; how to be all that God created me to be, or risk boldness, or lean in to an identity that is built only on truth. Being fully alive is much deeper, much richer, much harder than God wanting us to be happy. He wants us to be *alive*. Nothing shouts God's power, His goodness, or His redemption story louder than the life of a person who once was lost but now is found.

HEARING GOD'S VOICE
IN THE BEAUTY AROUND US

Read through these invitations to notice God in beauty. Which practice might help you listen for God's voice?

1. Engage with nature in a meaningful way. Even if you are in an urban environment, find a way to watch the sun rise or set or go to a park where you can be near trees. Go for a walk or just stay still. Whichever you choose, take a moment to journal what you see and what you hear.

2. Create something. What is God like as a Creator? How is that like or unlike your creative process? How can your creative efforts reflect that you bear God's image?

3. How do you express your love for God? Think of a way to uniquely express worship.

4. Do you know what makes you come alive? How does God delight in the true you, fully alive?

CHAPTER 10

A VOICE THAT SPEAKS IN DESIRING, WAITING, AND SILENCE

It was a question I did not have an answer to. My lips were dry, and the sun was relentless. The three of us sat facing each other, desperate, and without words for the first time in our friendship. Celebrating Michelle's birthday in Death Valley was either a subconscious decision or divine intervention. We were all breathing heavily, trying to inhale air in the desert.

Jessamyn, Michelle, and I have birthdays just a few months apart, and by the time Michelle turned thirty, we needed a reunion. We hopped on a plane for a short flight to Nevada, wearing sashes and tiaras and taking selfies in our seats. We laughed, amazed at how easy it was to slide into a vulnerable place of complete comfort with one another. We hadn't talked in far too long. A lot had changed since we were first friends. I got married, and Jessamyn tied the knot soon after. Michelle was still waiting for the right man. I had my first baby, and our Death Valley trip was my first night away from my squishy six-month-old daughter.

Jessamyn and I had been pregnant at the same time. She and I both went to breakfast with Michelle a year earlier, having the same secret glimmer in our eyes, the same too-early-for-most announcement to make. On the ride home we had excitedly declared names the other one wasn't allowed to claim, and I was thrilled to be pregnant, but I was near bursting to share this journey with my best friend.

Jessamyn's little baby should have been just a couple days younger than mine. Hers was an unimaginable loss. In the months that followed, I didn't know how to hold my joy and my best friend's grief at the same time, especially as the two emotions got tangled around a due date.

I hadn't been on a car ride with Jessamyn in far too long. She turned around from her passenger seat in the rental car and locked eyes with me as I sat in the back: "It must be hard to be away from your baby." I knew she wanted a baby more than anything in the world, but I could not have been happier to be away from mine. I was pretty sure good moms don't feel like that, and my heart beat faster in shame. It had become my darkest secret. I loved my baby, but I didn't like staying home with her. I wouldn't dare tell that to anyone. Definitely not to Jessamyn. Instead, I half smiled and said, "Thanks for asking. I know she is enjoying her daddy time."

It would not be long until the truth came out. All our truths spilled out. True stories need air, especially the ones that resist being told. Our deepest desires—the ones we work so hard to mute, to mask, and to ignore—were finally spoken.

Jessamyn wanted a baby.

Michelle wanted a husband.

I wanted a purpose—or at least an escape from purposelessness.

As the monsters of unmet desire cackled at our feet, the hopeless question came to us all at the same time. Finally someone asked *the question* in a hushed voice: "What if God never gives us what we want?"

After all, we weren't longing for God's biblical promises. We were longing after our own desires. And Desire was an accuser: she screamed that God didn't see, didn't care, wouldn't give. And Desire was close by. In fact, she felt even closer than God. Desire pointed to our hungry bellies and made us notice their growls.

Who was God to deny us satisfaction? But who were we to demand it from Him?

I had thought desire was a force within me that was at war with God's plan, so my job was to stop wanting things for myself and to want more of what God wanted. I could come before God's great white throne and lay everything I had ever hoped for before Him as a sacrifice. Then raise my chin and accept what He had for me instead, like trading a cupcake for a stick of celery. I simply had to learn what was good for me.

> God doesn't want us to give Him our desires and cringe at the thought of what He might give us in return. He wants to *be* our desire.

But God doesn't want us to give Him our desires and cringe at the thought of what He might give us in return. He wants to *be* our desire. He also wants us to be the kind of people who want and who love good things, who deeply love Him.

When I picture myself kneeling to lay my desires at the feet of God, I feel a towel brushing the soles of my upturned feet behind me. Even though every knee on heaven and earth will kneel at the name of Christ, one of His last acts on earth was to kneel and wash feet. Like Peter, I want to pull my feet away. *Stop! Not You! Lord, I am the one who serves You, not the other way around.* He robs me of my pious moment and firmly tells me that unless I let Him teach me, I will have no part of what He is doing.

And Jesus teaches me about desire.

Jesus washed His disciples' feet just a few days before His death. His spirit was troubled. He felt the fear, the anxiety, and the second-guessing that we all do when God calls us into the dark. Jesus went into that darkness anyway. His prayer in the garden, through sweat and blood and tears, is where He surrendered His desire to the Father: "My soul is very sorrowful, even to death. . . . My Father, if it be possible, let this cup pass from me; nevertheless, not as I will, but as you will" (Matthew 26:38–39 ESV).

Jesus taught us to pray the same thing in Matthew 6: "Your kingdom come, your will be done, on earth as it is in heaven" (v. 10). I have made my own self-righteous version of this and prayed it on more than one occasion:

Lord God, I really want this [boyfriend/job/house/school] . . . but it's not about what I want; it's about what You want. So I'll stop wanting it and wait to see what You give me instead, even if it means years of waiting and pain. Not my will, but Yours be done. Sincerely, Your devoted martyr, Liz. Amen. (P.S. If You were impressed by that prayer, feel free to give me what I originally wanted. I will definitely say thank You and give You the credit! XOXO!)

God doesn't want us to stop wanting; to lay our wants and our words of resignation at His feet. God is our good Father. He wants us to learn to want the right things. What we believe about God, do for God, or give to God barely scratches the surface of His design for our lives. What we love, whom we love, how we love, and the overflow of our spirit into words and actions matter a great deal more. God doesn't want us to stop wanting. He doesn't want our promises that we will accept whatever undesirable thing He has planned for us. "Your will; not mine" has always been a statement of trust and hope, of believing in God's good plan rather than dreading it. God wants us to desire His will because we believe He is good, His gifts are good, and His plans are good.

Jesus, though, questions our understanding of God as Father:

> Which one of you, if his son asks him for bread, will give him a stone? Or if he asks for a fish, will give him a serpent? If you then, who are evil, know how to give good gifts to your children, how much more will your Father who is in heaven give good things to those who ask him! (Matthew 7:9–11 ESV)

We assume God wants something for us that we will hate, as though He knows what is best for us, but He doesn't really know us at all. We have no problem casting God as an uncaring Father, ambivalent to our soul's deepest cries. Yet God designed us: He gave us quirks and gifts and talents and even desires. Our deepest desires for meaning, relationship, and purpose all lead us back to Him. They also cry out from the brokenness of our world in ache for the satisfaction of God's reality. If we dismiss our desires or sacrifice our desires, we will not be able to hear God's invitations in those desires. Jen Pollock Michel reminds us in *Teach Us to Want*:

> Although easily corrupted, desire is good, right and necessary. It is a force of movement in our lives, a means of transportation. It can be the very thing that motivates us to change and that carries us to God. Growing into maturity doesn't mean abandoning our desires, but growing in our discernment of them.

As the three of us sat in the desert with our desires out in the open, those wants continued staring us down. Our desires for family and love and purpose taunted us: God was not good for withholding, and we were not good for wanting. We did not know how to listen to those desires yet or how to honor their screeching cries. We hadn't learned to hold them tenderly skyward with upward-facing palms, not as a sacrifice to God but in desperation for His light to shine on them.

I've learned to pray a different prayer of desire since my time in the desert. No longer fearing God's response or anticipating suffering, I pray more vulnerably:

> *Lord God, I really want this [boyfriend/job/house/school] . . . sigh! . . . God, teach me what I really want. Reveal the ways I am looking for control, comfort, or acceptance in this situation. Help me to crave You instead. Free me from my bad motives and show me if there is anything left. Expose the dark corners of my soul that this desire illuminates. Show me what*

You want me to see in this heart-tug. I'm listening. What
You want for me is good and perfect and beautiful, so I want
what You want for me.

God has searched my desires many times now. He is teaching me to want good things, like working with Him and not just serving Him. To be excited about how He is forming my character instead of dreading what He might withhold from me. To trust that even when I don't get what I want, He is a God who feeds the ravens and knows what my family and I need. I am ashamed that I did not expect Him to be so tender.

A friend once told me that waiting in the meantime feels like such a mean time. She was right. We all left the desert empty-handed. Jessamyn wasn't pregnant, Michelle wasn't in love, and I was going home to a pile of laundry.

We all went home . . . and waited.

Waiting is an exercise of patience. The Chinese character for patience is phonetically pronounced "ren." The symbol is actually made up of two characters, a knife above a heart. That's what waiting feels like, our heart—our desires, dreams, health, life—threatened by a looming blade. Exposed to the danger of being hurt, extinguished, or nonexistent. I cannot help but squirm under that blade. Whenever I can, I try to avoid it altogether by giving up and not waiting or wanting. Abraham knew what it was like to have his whole heart sit under a blade, as his son Isaac squirmed under the blade he held. The Old Testament story of Abraham putting Isaac on an altar is incredibly confusing, since it seems to go against everything we know about the character of God. The author of Hebrews explains it to us: "Abraham reasoned that if

Isaac died, God was able to bring him back to life again. And in a sense, Abraham did receive his son back from the dead" (Hebrews 11:19 NLT).

The reason Abraham could confidently expose his heart—his greatest love, his only hope for the future, his only son with Sarah—to the blade of death was because he believed in resurrection. We, too, live with the hope of resurrection: we have seen Jesus embody the full power of God to restore life. When we are waiting, when being patient feels like a knife poised over our heart, we cannot forget the power of resurrection. Perhaps the knife will be removed, and the pain of waiting will give way to the sweet joy of our desire fulfilled. Even if the knife falls and the dream dies, God has a new life planned that we could never imagine.

We didn't know what we were waiting for, or where the knife would land. Michelle had no idea if she would ever get married and definitely no concept of how long she would be single. Jessamyn couldn't know if she would become a mother or how or when. I was less patient than either of them. Motherhood as a full-time job felt like a waste of my creative energy, so I went back to work just a couple weeks later.

We had all lost our ability to imagine what God might have for us if He didn't have the things we were waiting for. We did our best to lower our expectations and wait for God to hopefully do something. We had taken the desert home with us and carried its sand in our shoes.

I thought about the sand Israel wandered through in the desert for forty years with God. His provision felt miraculous in certain moments and disappointing other times. In the wilderness God might have seemed distant and uninvolved, yet He was doing some of His greatest work in and for us. Israel was making an idol as God was writing the Ten Commandments. Even as God was extending Himself in one of the most striking covenants of human history, He felt too far away. And we know that feeling that Marlena Graves put into words in *A Beautiful Disaster*: "In the wilderness, we remember that God did not bring us out here . . . to die. He brought us out to save us, to show us his power, to offer his comfort, and to put to death whatever is in us that is not of him."

The wilderness came before the promised land. It could have been time to heal after being slaves in Egypt, to write songs that declared salvation instead of lamenting slavery, or to savor manna like snowflakes on the tongue. Instead, the wilderness is where Israel and I both

> The reason Abraham could confidently expose his heart—his greatest love, his only hope for the future, his only son with Sarah—to the blade of death was because he believed in resurrection. We, too, live with the hope of resurrection.

end up angsty and complaining. Wilderness feels like wandering, but the wilderness always has a purpose. The wilderness humbled Nebuchadnezzar, focused John the Baptist, and proved the character of Jesus. God doesn't lead us into the wilderness to abandon us or punish us. He leads us to the wilderness to speak to us:

> "Therefore, behold, I will allure her,
>   and bring her into the wilderness,
>   and speak tenderly to her." (Hosea 2:14 ESV)

I wonder how waiting would feel if we believed the desert was a place we were invited, not abandoned. We will all find ourselves in a wilderness one day, deprived of our desire, hungry, and alone. Right where God wants to speak to us.

Truly, this time of waiting is one of grace, not torture. I do see you, wilderness dweller, tongue parched and eyes sunken. You cannot fathom what God is building in you right now. He is not withholding promises. He is actually building your endurance, refining your character, and strengthening your hope.

My friend Matt was the lead pastor of a church in another city. He had assumed responsibility for a struggling community of believers. He brought a strong vision and a clear strategy for turning things around. He felt God had asked him to take on this task, and Matt could identify ways he was uniquely gifted for this role. He was full of passion and energy and prayer when he started. When he showed up to a dinner two years later, his face was unshaven, his hands trembled, and his eyes were sleepless. He was waiting for a phone call. The elders were meeting to decide whether to fire him. Unsure if he even wanted his job anymore, he got tired of waiting and drove four hours to meet us around the table.

Instead of indulging our curiosity about the details, we asked Matt what the journey had been like for him. Matt's nose was facing the table, but his eyes looked up at us.

"Night. Dark night."

He recounted the sureness of his calling. But it was like Christ had walked him to the front door of that church and then left him utterly alone. He no longer heard God's voice, or easily recalled Scripture, or felt God's presence at all. Matt described it like walking up to an attic and expecting to discover interesting trunks and treasures, but instead finding the back of an old mirror with shattered glass everywhere. God had been edging nearer recently, without even a hint of divine apology.

My desire to be close to God is good, but that desire is not always holy. At the core, I enjoy God and the feeling of God's presence with me. I feel more confident and comforted when He answers my prayers. The darkness of my doubt stays at bay, its haunting and howling easily confused for the wind. If I am not vigilant, I could be motivated to be close to God out of sheer self-fulfillment.

That's why stories like Matt's as well as the ancient story of Job challenge me to the core. God has already seen through my attempts to manipulate and control Him. All my discipline and morality are tainted with self-interest. In His silence, He gently shows me, His eldest-son-type, approval-seeking, love-earning daughter. My faith stands naked and thin, clinging to God in an unloving dependence. In God's silence, I might experience less of Him, but I see more of me. My inflated convictions, deeper doubts, and willingness to quit. I surprise myself, disappoint myself, and want to hide myself.

The story of Job in the Old Testament describes a good man who loves God, loves his family, and does good in his community. As the story unfolds, God allows Job to be tested by Satan. Job passes his horrific test with flying colors. God's joy and confidence in Job are so strong He allows Job to be tested again. Until the end of the story, God is completely silent. Job has no idea why God has abandoned him to misery or what he did to deserve this. Silence tests and proves us; God is not the One on trial. We may be tempted to drag God into court over His abandonment, but we see in Job's story and many others that God is far more present, aware, and active in His silence than we realize.

It is dangerous to assume the only reason someone might feel distant from God is as a result of sin. Job was a perfectly righteous man whose friends accused him instead of accompanying him through the dark. It would also be wrong to always assume that God's silence is never a consequence of our sin. Although it is not our place to judge the hearts of others, and it is dangerous for us to assume silence is always a result of sin, sin can create a barrier, muffling the magnetic pull of God. If we see that effect in our own lives, forgiveness is as close as "I'm sorry."

> Listen! The LORD's arm is not too weak to save you,
>   nor is his ear too deaf to hear you call.
> It's your sins that have cut you off from God.
>   Because of your sins, he has turned away
>   and will not listen anymore. (Isaiah 59:1–2 NLT)

If you are wandering in the meantime of waiting, God is with you. He has something tender to say to you here and a profound purpose for what may seem like wasted time. The promised land will be sweet, but God is not withholding good things from you now. He has good things for you, and He is doing good things in you, right there in the wilderness of waiting.

Three years after Death Valley, the three of us would adventure again, this time in the fertile Yosemite Valley. You would barely recognize us. We were much older than three years could justify.

I was finally comfortable being slow and quiet in my own stretched and tired skin.

Jessamyn was strong and joyful . . . and pregnant.

Michelle was radiant from the inside out, her eyes sparkling like the ring on her finger. We were all in Yosemite for her wedding. The day before the ceremony, we went for a hike. It was only a few miles before we were stopped in our tracks. Nevada Falls is nearly six hundred feet high, and we were so close that the mist was soaking our faces. A rainbow wrapped itself around that waterfall, and a good God whispered His ancient promise, "I will not destroy you."

God is for us and not against us, and He faithfully keeps His promises to love us and be with us always, both in the desert and in the rain of blessing. We instinctively reached out to grab one another's hands. We prayed. We were quicker to pray now, less prone to just talk about prayer. We were so thankful, sincerely and unquestioningly grateful. We asked God to protect and grow the baby Jessamyn held inside her. We thanked Him for His faithfulness, and we leaned in and trusted His faithfulness more. No more fear for the mystery on the horizon. As we prayed, the wet spray rained on our eyelashes and seeped into our clothes: we stood in the showers of hope.

> God promises always to be with us to the end of the earth. He sees us, cares for us, and is active in our lives even when we cannot see Him, feel Him, or have any sense of what He is doing.

For every second that we stood in the splash of the rainbow, sure of God's promises, we had each spent sleepless hours tossing in the dark of night. Unsure if God could hear our prayers at all.

But God is communicating to each of us even when He seems silent. Silence is nakedness; the vulnerability is as uncomfortable as it is intimate. God promises always to be with us to the end of the earth. He sees us, cares for us, and is active in our lives even when we cannot see Him, feel Him, or have any sense of what He is doing. The night comes.

Times of wilderness can often be looked back on and understood or appreciated in hindsight. Times of silence are not so tidy. Times of wilderness can come after times of great celebration. The rescue of Israel from Egypt and Jesus's baptism were both followed by the wilderness. Times of silence are more often triggered by grief and struggle. That was the experience of C. S. Lewis, as he wrote about in *A Grief Observed*:

> Go to [God] when your need is desperate, when all other help is vain, and what do you find? A door slammed in your face, and a sound of bolting and double bolting on the inside. After that, silence. You may as well turn away. The longer you wait, the more emphatic the silence will become. There are no lights in the windows. It might be an empty house. Was it ever inhabited? It seemed so once. And that seeming was as strong as this. What can this mean? Why is He so present a commander in our time of prosperity and so very absent a help in time of trouble?

In his book *Hearing God*, Dallas Willard describes a godly woman who worried. She had heard a story of God speaking in a clear and direct way to her pastor, and she realized she had never heard God that way. In fact, He seemed quite silent. God's voices can definitely be hard to recognize if you expect them to sound a certain way. The absence of God's audible voice is certainly not His silence; He might be speaking to you in a hundred other ways.

Silence does not always have to be painful or mysterious. Silence can be beautifully intimate. The silence that we offer to God and the silence He offers to us can be places of rest and safety. Once we no longer fear silence and we practice it daily, it can amplify God's voice. Think about a first date: a couple might be talking over each other, asking eager questions and giving hopeful responses. When a couple is finally comfortable with one another, they can happily be with one another, fully present, even without words.

When we prayed under the waterfall for Jessamyn to have a healthy baby, we asked her how she felt. She confessed that she had prayed for three years in cold silence from God, but she was still praying. Somehow she had not run out of tears or breath or hope.

We waited and prayed with bated breath through the summer, struggling to trust God to intervene. Fighting every self-protective instinct within us. And choosing hope. Jessamyn's baby shower was six months later. God's long silence was finally broken. After all the doubt and fear, the awareness of love and blessing was a higher high, following as it did the lowest low. Our friend Jeannie Whitlock didn't know about the desert or the waterfall, but she knew Jessamyn. She wrote this poem that was read at the baby shower:

The farmer ploughs cracked earth,
The bobcat paces a shrinking pool,
And the long road of trust—curves;
Til, over browning mountains, gray begins
To pile and roll, and every leaf trembles in the gathering cool,
And the smell of hot pavement changes, and on the wind

The first drops come—
Then a patter—
Then a flood;
Yours is the joy of storm clouds burst open!
The joy of the deluge, the joy of drought broken;
Laughing, we splash in puddles where dust had lain;
Drenched in His downpouring love,
We drink it in,
We dance with you, sister, in the rain!

In God's silence our faith is tested; our misalignment, exposed; our trust, strengthened; and our intimacy, proved. You see, just as the physically blind find that their other senses are heightened, God's seeming absence from our emotions can teach us to recognize Him with our will, our mind, or other ways. Our thoughts, feelings, and sensations can be heightened or dulled, but our own experience of God does not define Him. He will always be *I AM*. He will always be loving and working and remaking us and our world.

God used four hundred years of silence to prepare His people for Jesus Christ, the most tangible expression of His presence with us since the beginning of time. God has a purpose for silence in our lives as well.

HEARING GOD'S VOICE IN DESIRE, WAITING, AND SILENCE

Read through these invitations to notice God's desire, waiting, and silence. Which practice might help you listen for God's voice?

1. Make a list of everything you want right now, the big things and the small things. What stray thoughts have been crossing your mind about vacations, promotions, relationships, clothing, achievement, cars, houses, goals for your kids, etc.? Record a list on the side of a page.
   - Bring this list to God and ask Him to help you understand your truest desires. Look for the ways your desires may reflect human longings for safety, control, approval, purpose, or pain control. Ask God how your desires are pushing you away from Him and which desires He gave you are pulling you toward Him.

2. When God's people doubt Him, He consistently points to His faithfulness in the past as proof that celebration will come again. So take a blank sheet of paper and draw a line that represents your life. Mark your line with times when God brought joy, blessing, strength, or good experiences into your life. Place stars along the line for when God put people in your life who made a positive impact on you. As you remember God's goodness in your story, think of a creative way to thank Him through art, music, dance, or a thank-You card.

3. Offer God five minutes of silence every morning this week. Find a quiet place and eliminate as much noise as possible. Read Psalm 63:1–8 to begin your time. As thoughts and distractions arise in the silence, do not fight them. Acknowledge their presence and then imagine you are "swiping left" to dismiss them from your mind screen. Or imagine these thoughts moving past you like ships down a river or items on a conveyor belt.

4. Reflect on your time of silence. What thoughts, emotions, or reactions did the silence prompt? What can you do to help silence become a place where you notice God and sit comfortably with Him?

EPILOGUE

Eddy was always standing in the church doorway on Sunday evenings, white-haired and hunched over a bit, wearing a plaid sport coat and shaking every hand. He was the Willy Wonka of my childhood, with his bottomless pockets of butterscotch candy.

One evening when I walked up to claim my piece of gold, he scrutinized my eight-year-old frame with a raised eyebrow. In my hurry to leave the house, I had forgotten my veil. Eddy silently pulled a cardboard box from the bookshelf beside him and set it before me like a tray of chocolates. It was overflowing with colorful mismatched scarves and lace triangles, some threadbare, a heap of musty smelling cheap nylon. Eddy watched me fasten the scarf in a knot at the base of my neck before he let my mother and me pass.

The church basement was somber in the dusk of evening as we all returned only a few hours after morning services had let out. The bowl of red punch with its giant ice cube had been washed and put away. No one was marveling over Jada's giant earrings, and she wasn't telling the story of how her name in sign language is a big swoosh below the earlobe (because of her amazing earrings). Earlier this afternoon the old men had seized running children as a bear plucks salmon from the river, but everyone moved quietly now. A square ripple of rows all faced the table in the center that was set every week with bread and juice. Next to those sacred elements were red velvet bags, with golden cords that looked like king's purses. The offering bag was all I could see. My clammy fingers choked the top of a flimsy fold-over sandwich bag that held a fistful of loose change. It was all the treasure I had, and tonight was the night I was giving it to God.

During the Breaking of Bread, the women and girls sat in complete silence as we did at all the other services. I rolled the butterscotch candy over my tongue and let it click against the back of my teeth. If I ate it too quickly, I would not have anything to use my mouth for.

All of the women sat quietly with their veils on, most taking care not to draw attention to themselves, but Jada always had a veil with bright yellows and purples and orange. During the morning service, she stood at the lower left-hand side of the stage, translating the message into ASL for the row of deaf men and women who leaned toward her. Sometimes she hunched her shoulders as if she were whispering, sometimes waving her arms as if she were being attacked. I watched her rouse smiles and laughs from her silent row when I should have been paying attention to the drone of the speaker behind the pulpit. All the women were silent, but when Jada moved her hands, she had a voice. Tonight was Jada's turn to worship. Her eyes moved back and forth beneath her closed eyelids, her body gently rocking. The deaf didn't come to the Breaking of Bread; they took Communion in the morning.

Jada wrapped her veil around her head instead of letting it drape over her shoulders. No one ever corrected her. Mine was much more simple and modest, a sheer black square with little white flowers. Our veils showed our submission to our fathers, to the elders, and to God "so that all the angels could see." I started wearing a veil around the time I started kindergarten, and I don't remember ever being at church without mine on. Tonight my head itched, and I was scratching at the knot at the back of the scarf I had borrowed. This veil wasn't as soft as mine.

There were always long stretches of silence in this service, something I later learned came from a Quaker influence. The men would stand up occasionally, as the Spirit led them, and share a thought or a verse or a hymn. About the cross. About the blood. The lucky kids got to bring coloring books. I spent my time staring.

Mr. Benzinger took up almost an entire row with his wife, his au pair, and the six Benzinger children. None of us kids had first names, only last names. Mr. Benzinger wore a straightly buttoned, short-sleeved shirt every week, and you could always smell the starch in his sleeves and see the undershirt he wore beneath it. Thick black glasses and dark hair were a stark contrast to his pale white skin and crystalline blue eyes. All of his kids were home-schooled, and all of them were afraid of him, so I was afraid of him too. They said he made their au pair dig a ditch for the sprinklers, and she had called her mom in Germany. But her mom wouldn't let her come home till the summer was over. I watched the au pair's face with curiosity as though I could perceptively settle the ditch-digging rumor right there. She wasn't sad or scared; she was blank. I thought it meant nothing, but now I know it meant everything. A mauve scarf covered her light brown hair and blended her features into one another. I'm sad I can't remember her name. Only Mr. Benzinger's.

While I was busy counting the stars on the American flag that hung in the corner, my dad stood up beside me. The bottom of his chair make a dull scraping noise in the silence as his calves pushed the chair back. Everyone listened when he spoke. He was tall, charismatic, and the youngest leader of our Assembly. Mrs. Murphy said he looked like Mark Hamill. I didn't know who that was, but she said it like it was a good thing, and my dad liked to repeat it. I studied Dad's jaw from below. When he got emotional, his jaw would tighten shut and his lips would barely separate as he talked. He was one of the few men in the room who ever seemed genuinely sad that Jesus died.

I scrambled for the thin yellow songbook while he was talking, his leather Bible splayed open and falling over both sides of his hand, bobbing gently up and down above my head. I frantically flipped the pages to the song about the deer panting by the water, my absolute favorite. I held it out low in front of me, slyly pointing to the song number. It could have been Christmas Day or my birthday. It didn't matter. Dad always wanted to sing "How Great Thou Art."

I set the songbook down and found the illustration that I had been staring at all week in my pale pink children's Bible. It had a caption that read "God loves a cheerful giver" with a huge-headed, wide-eyed cherub child and his puppy. As the loaf of bread came by, I passed it to my father without taking a bite, and as the tray of juice thimbles came down the row, my heart quickened. The offering was next.

Someone prayed something, and I knew my moment was coming. I reached under my chair to grab my bag of coins, letting it jingle a little. I remembered Jesus in the temple praising the widow for her penny offering and the little strange-headed Precious

Moments boy with his puppy as I clutched my pennies proudly, cheerfully. My feet didn't hit the floor as they dangled from the chair, and I pulled the pennies out one,

by one,

by one,

when suddenly, with one movement of frustration, my dad grabbed the plastic bag from my hand and tossed it in the offering purse. He quickly passed the red velvet bag down the row, and I only saw the back of his dark-haired head nodding to the man beside him as if to apologize.

Though I haven't been near that basement for many years, it still occasionally forms the backdrop of my dreams. I hover over it, like a ghost, but as I remember my past, it's the people in the room who are finally hazier than I. That sweet little girl, so desperate for a seat at the Communion table. No bag of coins can buy her a place.

Decades later, on a foggy Sunday morning, we gathered in a circle around a small table in the loft of an Alaskan fishing lodge. The table was also set with bread and a single goblet of wine instead of all the tiny plastic cups. A dozen of us were away from our normal churches, and we wanted to remember Jesus and remind each other of His body that was broken for us, His blood that was shed for us. It cost Christ all of heaven to put on that body, and then He gave it up. We sang hymns and songs to remember the significance of the cross. The a cappella harmony of "How Great Thou Art," the shape of the circle, and the elements in the center unexpectedly prompted a flood of memories that took me back to the darkness of the basement.

As I looked up from the tears I could not fight back, the person next to me kindly extended a cup of deep purple and a cracked loaf of bread to me on a tray. With soft eyes, the person sitting beside me offered the elements, inviting me to "take and eat."

I was finally sitting at the kind of table God has in His home, one where everyone is invited to feast on mercy and grace. I thought I had been on a journey all this time to find my voice, but really it was a journey to find His.

There was a time I would have seized that box of mismatched scarves by Eddy's basement door and used it to fuel a bonfire that might consume that memory. But every story needs a beginning, so I reach into the haze instead to grab the most colorful scarves from the box, the ones that remind me of Jada. I place a few into the scarred hands of Jesus, who is standing beside me, so that He and I can throw them high into the air, fling them into each other's faces like snowballs, and laugh in the freedom that none of those ghosts know they could have. Not even the little girl with her bag of coins.

"It is for freedom that Christ has set us free," Paul proclaimed in Galatians 5:1. From God's earliest promise to Abraham, we understand that the freedom God has for His people is a freedom meant to be shared.

In hearing God's voice, I found my own. His love gave me confidence to speak out despite my insecurity. His healing broke the silence of my deepest pain. His goodness cried "be still" to the waves of grief that had attacked and receded for years. God's words offer so much more than comfort, wisdom, or even trajectory for your life. They will form the ongoing conversation you have with Him, they'll shape the way you experience the world, and they will fill you to overflowing with an abundant life of love. Love for God, love for your friends and family, love for complete strangers, and even love for your enemies.

From as far back as I can remember, I had yearned to belong with God at His table. Sometimes I felt blocked out by people, while at other times I got in my own way, but finally I know what it is like to eat with God. It's not just a table set for two; it's a feast for everyone. God gives us words not only for ourselves, but He speaks to us so that we can speak to others (2 Corinthians 1:3–4). Your invitation to eat with God and to speak with God was meant to be accepted so that you can enjoy what God has for you, and also so you can invite others to His table (Luke 14:13).

In 1 Corinthians 11:23–26 Paul explained the way he understood Communion: eating the bread and drinking the wine is an imperative given by Christ. It is both a remembrance and a proclamation. Different church traditions have

> God's words offer so much more than comfort, wisdom, or even trajectory for your life. They will form the ongoing conversation you have with Him.

practiced and protected the act of Communion in different ways. For some believers, it matters very much who serves and who eats Communion. Many think of Communion as a ritual of the church that is exclusive to those who belong through faith, catechism, baptism, membership, or another sign of belief.

In reading the Corinthians passage, I was struck by the words *remembrance* and *proclaim*. There is no greater symbol of the gospel than the cross and no experience of the cross more physical than the bread and wine. Jesus was artful in His use of imagery to connect us with the greater truths of God, and the bread and wine He puts before us are an invitation to participate in His death and ultimately His resurrection.

When I was invited to serve Easter Communion in the jail with the other chaplains, at first I wasn't sure about participating. I have always thought of Communion as a practice of worship in the church, and in our church context we ask people who are not followers of Christ to rest and reflect rather than to participate in that part of the service. I talked to the main chaplain, and she smiled.

"Everything looks different in here," she said.

We were going to be giving the opportunity to some sisters in Christ to participate in this sacred ritual that they do not always have access to. In some cases, the inmates have very limited contact with the outside world. The bread and juice come to them through a small hole in their door, yet the reminder of grace still finds them. Of course, not everyone who would participate would be a believer. Christ didn't ask us to police that, not even on a Sunday morning in a polite church setting. We are simply called to remember and proclaim. Having used many visuals for the gospel over the years, I was struck by how perfect the bread and cup are. After praying about it and asking for advice, I decided to join the team of chaplains and offer bread and juice to the inmates who wanted to participate during Holy Week. For some it would be a traditional Communion, but for others it would be remembering and proclaiming the love of Christ for the first time.

I met with the chaplains, and we prayed in our office, overcrowded with donated books that have all the staples and hardcovers removed from them. Days before Easter, I thought of Christ during His final week. His agony, His betrayal, His determination, and His faithful love. Remembering His cross and proclaiming its power felt particularly significant in these walls. This jail was a place that needed to be reminded that death has been defeated.

Two other chaplains and I stood in the center of a cement room. There were two levels of rooms that looked into the center. The guard knocked on every door, a quick *rap-rap*. "Chaplains are here. Do you want to take Communion?"

Slowly the women trickled out of their rooms. Some sleepy. Some curious. All stretching their arms and legs. They gathered around us in a large circle. I hadn't planned what I was going to say, but the other two chaplains looked at me, so I began to talk about Jesus. All the words of the Gospels that I had been meditating on that week took over. I told them the story of how Jesus was anointed for His death, not by a priest but by a woman whom everyone else thought was unworthy. I told them about how Jesus's friends scattered in the garden when the authorities came. I retold the story of Jesus's trial and how He watched silently as other people testified against Him, all of them lying.

As the words kept coming, faces softened, tears rolled down cheeks, and eyes looked to the floor. I was talking, but the Holy Spirit was connecting the story of Jesus to the experiences of these women in ways I could only imagine. There was so much pain in their eyes. I now know the face of the man who hung on a cross beside Jesus. Who realized he deserved his punishment but that Christ did not.

As I described Christ's days leading to the cross, I recognized that these women have a shared experience with Christ that I struggle to understand during Holy Week. They know what it is like to be abandoned. They know what it is like to be condemned. I have seen Christ meet these women in their pain again and again, but for the first time I saw them meet Christ in *His* pain. These incredible women led me to Jesus with them as the cement walls and their wet eyes reminded me that I was once a condemned prisoner as well. I too easily forget that I wasn't just lost without Christ; I was as good as dead.

We eat this bread because we know Your body was broken for us.

We drink this juice because we remember Your blood was shed on the cross.

We proclaim today—and until You come again, Jesus—that death could not claim You. That because of Your resurrection, we can all walk through death and have life in You. Only by Your grace. Only by Your name.

My favorite gathering at the Lord's Table was the one I almost didn't show up for. When I did, I realized I am not on a journey to belonging, but that I already belong. I'm in Christ's story now, and we are all about extending belonging to others. His words have never been just for me; they've always been for all of us. His Spirit doesn't breathe into my body so I can talk louder or truer; it's so I can talk more like my Father. I have been so angry and indignant when I felt my voice was unheard, I haven't even thought about how many times I've ignored what God was trying to say to me. It's not until I learned to listen that I had anything to say. In finding God's voice, we will find our own.

As you hear God's words and respond to them, may you carry His whispers of love, hope, acceptance, and belonging with you everywhere you go.

ACKNOWLEDGMENTS

What no one told me about writing a book was how hard it was going to be, or how many times I was going to want to quit, or how each deadline would feel impossible to meet. No one told me I was going to need so many people helping and loving and believing in me to keep me from throwing my laptop into the lake. I didn't plan ahead, but the people I needed were there anyway.

My husband, Mike Ditty, is not just a mandatory thank you. He's the reason you are reading this book. He's the one who sent me in to the woods to write and picked up the slack at home while I was gone. Then, even knowing how hard that was, he did it again and again. He's the one who held my fear and my insecurity and my tired body when I fell into his arms and was sure I was failing. He's the one who loves our kids and me so well, who listens to our dreams and treasures them along with us—taking them more seriously than we might dare. Thank you, honey.

It is entirely ridiculous how much of my life I spend feeling a little lonely or disconnected, because all evidence points the opposite way. I have a gluttony of phenomenal friends. Thank you to my many friends who trusted me to tell your stories; I saw God more clearly because of you: Jessamyn Kirkwood, Michelle Vitus, Julia Paulsen, Lisa Averill, Andy Gridley, and all of you who discovered yourself on these pages. Thank you to the friends who wrote me cards along the way. I still have each one and have always carried them in my laptop bag and have read them at least a dozen times. To the friends who made me "writer snacks," you know tea and dates fuel me as well as handwritten cards, and I felt so seen and loved and fed by you. David Kim, Josh Fox, Aleah Marsden, Bronwyn Lea, and other early chapter readers, thank you for your honesty and perspective. Steve Clifford . . . that phone call—I won't forget it.

To my Grit Group, Aleah and Bronwyn, I'm deeply thankful for our daily sharing of writerly struggles and occasional sharing of monumental victories. Our adventures are so much better when shared. To my cohort at the Harvester Island Wilderness Workshop, and specifically Leslie Leyland Fields and Philip Yancey, thank you for teaching me how to write a book. To my Redbud Writer's Guild, thank you for the opportunity to write, learn, practice, grow, and be connected through you all. Thank you to my agent, Don Gates, and The Gates Group Literary Agency, for taking a chance on me and my words. I've been so grateful for Worthy Publishing and the strong team that they placed behind this book, including my editor, Kyle Olund.

Now before I thank God, can I make a confession? I was haunted by a fear since almost the very beginning of this process, that the moment I set out to write about God's voice He would certainly go silent on me. That I would feel like an imposter and be forced to write in the dark. Although God does speak through silence, that wasn't even close to what He had in mind. He has been closer and kinder than I ever dreamed; and writing this book in the midst of His unfolding miracles and gifts of light has been the adventure of a lifetime. Thank you, Lord, for this fantastic invitation to do something with You that was entirely beyond me.

ABOUT THE AUTHOR

LIZ DITTY is on the teaching team at Westgate Church, a multi-site nondenominational church in California's Silicon Valley. She also preaches at other local churches and loves speaking to women, millennials, college students, MOPs groups, and others through Bible studies, conferences, and retreats.

Liz is a trained spiritual director through the Sustainable Faith (sustainablefaith.com) program and believes we can all see God more clearly when we look for Him in the stories that surround our everyday life. In addition to *God's Many Voices*, her writing has been published in the Campus Crusade anthology *Dating During the Apocalypse* and on several Christian women's websites.

Liz and her husband live in San Jose and love exploring the Bay Area trails and parks with their two young kids. Her two little ones may have thrown her corporate trajectory for a loop, but they've taught her to sing (badly), dance (awkwardly), and laugh (loudly) more than she ever thought she would.

LizDitty.com

IF YOU ENJOYED THIS BOOK, WILL YOU CONSIDER SHARING THE MESSAGE WITH OTHERS?

Mention the book in a blog post or through Facebook, Twitter, Pinterest, or upload a picture through Instagram.

Recommend this book to those in your small group, book club, workplace, and classes.

Head over to facebook.com/lizdittycom, "LIKE" the page, and post a comment as to what you enjoyed the most.

Post a picture of the book on Instagram with the caption: "I recommend reading #GodsManyVoices by @lizditter // @worthypub"

Pick up a copy for someone you know who would be challenged and encouraged by this message.

Write a book review online.

Visit us at worthypublishing.com

twitter.com/worthypub

instagram.com/worthypub

facebook.com/worthypublishing

youtube.com/worthypublishing